The Kentucky Bicentennial Bookshelf
Sponsored by

KENTUCKY HISTORICAL EVENTS CELEBRATION COMMISSION
KENTUCKY FEDERATION OF WOMEN'S CLUBS

and Contributing Sponsors

AMERICAN FEDERAL SAVINGS & LOAN ASSOCIATION
ARMCO STEEL CORPORATION, ASHLAND WORKS
A. ARNOLD & SON TRANSFER & STORAGE CO., INC. / ASHLAND OIL, INC.
BAILEY MINING COMPANY, BYPRO, KENTUCKY / BEGLEY DRUG COMPANY
J. WINSTON COLEMAN, JR. / CONVENIENT INDUSTRIES OF AMERICA, INC.
IN MEMORY OF MR. AND MRS. J. SHERMAN COOPER BY THEIR CHILDREN
CORNING GLASS WORKS FOUNDATION / MRS. CLORA CORRELL
THE COURIER-JOURNAL AND THE LOUISVILLE TIMES
COVINGTON TRUST & BANKING COMPANY
MR. AND MRS. GEORGE P. CROUNSE / GEORGE E. EVANS, JR.
FARMERS BANK & CAPITAL TRUST COMPANY / FISHER-PRICE TOYS, MURRAY
MARY PAULINE FOX, M.D., IN HONOR OF CHLOE GIFFORD
MARY A. HALL, M.D., IN HONOR OF PAT LEE,
JANICE HALL & MARY ANN FAULKNER
OSCAR HORNSBY INC. / OFFICE PRODUCTS DIVISION IBM CORPORATION
JERRY'S RESTAURANTS / ROBERT B. JEWELL
LEE S. JONES / KENTUCKIANA GIRL SCOUT COUNCIL
KENTUCKY BANKERS ASSOCIATION / KENTUCKY COAL ASSOCIATION, INC.
THE KENTUCKY JOCKEY CLUB, INC. / THE LEXINGTON WOMAN'S CLUB
LINCOLN INCOME LIFE INSURANCE COMPANY
LORILLARD A DIVISION OF LOEW'S THEATRES, INC.
METROPOLITAN WOMAN'S CLUB OF LEXINGTON / BETTY HAGGIN MOLLOY
MUTUAL FEDERAL SAVINGS & LOAN ASSOCIATION
NATIONAL INDUSTRIES, INC. / RAND MCNALLY & COMPANY
PHILIP MORRIS, INCORPORATED / MRS. VICTOR SAMS
SHELL OIL COMPANY, LOUISVILLE
SOUTH CENTRAL BELL TELEPHONE COMPANY
SOUTHERN BELLE DAIRY CO. INC.
STANDARD OIL COMPANY (KENTUCKY)
STANDARD PRINTING CO., H. M. KESSLER, PRESIDENT
STATE BANK & TRUST COMPANY, RICHMOND
THOMAS INDUSTRIES INC. / TIP TOP COAL CO., INC.
MARY L. WISS, M.D. / YOUNGER WOMAN'S CLUB OF ST. MATTHEWS

The Kentucky Shakers

JULIA NEAL

THE UNIVERSITY PRESS OF KENTUCKY

Research for The Kentucky Bicentennial Bookshelf
is assisted by a grant from the
National Endowment for the Humanities.
Views expressed in the Bookshelf do not
necessarily represent those of the Endowment.

ISBN: 0-8131-0236-7

Library of Congress Catalog Card Number: 76-46029

A statewide cooperative scholarly publishing agency
serving Berea College, Centre College of Kentucky,
Eastern Kentucky University, The Filson Club,
Georgetown College, Kentucky Historical Society,
Kentucky State University, Morehead State University,
Murray State University, Northern Kentucky University,
Transylvania University, University of Kentucky,
University of Louisville, and Western Kentucky University.

Editorial and Sales Offices: Lexington, Kentucky 40506

TO
Eldress Bertha Lindsey
of the Canterbury Shakers
who has the gift to be simple
and
who is what she seems

Contents

Preface

PASSING INSTITUTIONS in America seem to receive more attention than do living ones. So today when the Shaker rolls have been closed since 1957 and when there are only ten sisters and no brother in the two remaining eastern societies, there has come the inevitable upsurge of interest in all things Shaker.

Such an interest results in sincere attempts to save and study the Shaker heritage, but it also spawns much that is spurious. Many superficial articles are being rushed to the popular periodicals. Much country furniture is suddenly being labeled Shaker.

Hoping to avoid error, repetitiveness, and generalities, I have gone to the original Shaker manuscripts and have, as far as possible, let the Pleasant Hill and South Union Shakers tell their own story.

To read the primary Shaker records is to realize that the Kentucky Shaker scribes were as honest and forthright in using the language as they were in turning the native stone and clay into exemplary buildings and the native woods into functional furniture. Today at the two restored Kentucky Shakertowns—one in Mercer County, and one in Logan— much of the Shaker heritage remains to be seen and admired.

1

COMING TO THE WESTERN COUNTRY

IT WAS MARCH 1, 1805, when three Shakers from New Lebanon, New York—John Meacham, Benjamin Seth Youngs, and Issachar Bates—walked into Garrard County, Kentucky. The few early signs of spring showing along the creeks and valleys must have looked good to the men who had been walking for eight weeks through rigorous winter weather.

Finding a "decent, modest" house, the travelers took lodging, washed their clothes, and spent the evening asking their hosts about the current religious excitement in the Paint Lick area. Doubtless they told their hosts how some twenty-five years earlier there had been a great religious revival in New England. During that time converts had been attracted to a new faith held by people who called themselves United Believers in the Second Appearing of Christ and later were to be known as Shakers.

John Meacham may have spoken of his father, Joseph Meacham, a Baptist minister who had turned to the new Shaker faith and had later become the first American convert to be appointed head of the Shaker organization, a position he kept until his death in 1796.

Because the visitors showed such interest in the revival matters, the Kentuckians invited them to attend services next day

1

at Matthew Houston's Presbyterian meetinghouse and to join in an evening society meeting in Houston's home. Later Bates wrote in his journal that Benjamin "spoke some" at the society meeting, but it was not until the following Thursday, March 6, at a second such meeting that these "singular people" opened their first full public "testimony in the West."

At that time the Shakers said they approved of the revival "as far as it went," but they "signified" they had something more and better than anything the revivalists had yet experienced. Stating that they had come to teach the full gospel, the easterners began to outline the main Shaker tenets. First they explained that Shakers did not count anything their own, but kept all things in common, stressing that every Shaker was expected to work with his own hands to provide things "honest in the sight of men," and "to lay up in store provisions for the honor of God and the relief and succor of him that needeth."

They explained that among the Shakers no poor man had to stand aside so that a rich man could be seated in a good place. Furthermore, equality was extended to women, for had not Christ appeared the second time in the woman Ann Lee? And it was she who had led the Shakers, or Believers in the Second Appearing of Christ, from England to the American colonies in 1774. They explained that the church covenant called for the appointment of eldresses as well as elders, for elder sisters as well as for elder brothers.

They spoke also of how one must confess his sins to another Christian witness. And they spoke of celibacy. Celibacy, they said, meant that covenant members were expected to live as brothers and sisters, not as husbands and wives. The speaker admitted, however, that although covenant Shakers were to be celibate and thus center all their attention on spiritual matters, they knew that others were "not called therein."

A few days later the three visitors, wearing their broad-brimmed hats and their long black coats, set out for Bourbon County to visit the site of the great Cane Ridge camp meeting. They had been told in Paint Lick that at Cane Ridge "the people know more about these things." They had also been told that some of the revivalists were practicing a new form of worship, engaging in singular bodily exercises such as dancing and jerking, barking and rolling. Also they had heard that the entire congregation sometimes prayed aloud with such power and volume of sound that they could be heard at a great distance. These deviates from the conventional denominations were called New Lights.

Traveling through Lexington, the men arrived on March 13 in the Cane Ridge home of the minister Barton Stone, who invited them "for much conversation" with him and a number more. Stone thought the appearance of the men was "humble and interesting." Later he described their appearance as being "prepossessing" and their dress "plain and neat." He found the men "grave and unassuming, very intelligent and ready in the Scriptures and to have a great boldness in their faith." In fact, Stone wrote his colleague John Dunlavy that he "was never so completely swallowed up with any man as with Issachar Bates, while he opened the testimony" and that he was "pleased with Shaker testimony until they came on marriage."

In his autobiography, Bates wrote of that first Cane Ridge visit, noting that "the people sucked in our light as greedily as ever an ox drank water and all wondered where they had been and not seen these things before." But he had to admit that the minister Barton Stone was not so ready "to take up the very cross of Christ and enter into the same self-denying path of regeneration." Satan entered into Stone, "who set more store by his Eliza than by all the salvation that God had prepared for the fallen race." But Stone seemed friendly and "desired us, at least one of us, to attend their next camp meeting which we agreed to do."

During their two days in Cane Ridge the visitors learned that the revival fires that had ignited first in Logan County on the Gasper, Muddy, and Red rivers in 1798–1800 had been spreading throughout central and northern Kentucky and were at that time burning brightly across the Ohio River.

Crossing over into the Miami River territory, the three Shakers went first to Springdale or Springfield and sought out John Thompson, "who had given the New Lights their name." The men wanted to talk to Thompson, a former Presbyterian who had begun in 1804 to advocate praising God in the dance. He might prove a willing hearer of Shaker doctrine.

It is apparent that the three easterners made it their practice to seek out all the most prominent revival ministers. In Kentucky they had spent time with Matthew Houston and Barton Stone. In Ohio they sought out not only Thompson but also Richard McNemar and John Dunlavy. It proved to be good strategy, because Houston, McNemar, and Dunlavy accepted the Shaker faith and brought a large part of their congregations with them. No doubt the Shakers were disappointed when Thompson became an archenemy who proclaimed that he could see "the mark of the beast on that church" as plain as he could see "the paper on which he wrote."

When Bates returned to Cane Ridge two weeks later, he went to Stone's house and found the leading New Light preachers already assembled. Among these were Robert Marshall and John Thompson. These men, along with Stone and others, received Bates with only "outward kindness." But when the people showed great friendliness, the New Light leaders were "struck with great fear and concluded that the Shakers should not be permitted to speak for fear of conquering the people." On the third day, however, the ministers reluctantly consented to dismiss their service at noon in order that the Shaker brother could speak. "And I did so," wrote Bates.

For several days following the meeting, Bates visited from house to house. Many of the people he visited said the Shakers were right. Many reported having visions. One young man said he saw three patches of flax. One represented the Presbyterians and it was nearly all rape. The second was the Methodists and that one was about two-thirds rape. But the third was the SHAKERS and it was all clean flax.

Although the reported dreams and many conversations favored Shakerism, Bates observed that there was an "abominable Stone bridge the people were afraid to cross" and a "bull in the gap that would not go through, nor would he allow others to go."

4

It seems ironic that when Bates returned to Ohio, he was carrying a letter from Stone to Richard McNemar, in which Stone had written, "Most Dear Brother, inform me what you think of these men among you from a distant region."

A few weeks later when Stone learned that his "dear brother" had espoused the Shaker doctrines, he asserted his enmity and denounced Shakerism both from the preaching stands and in the press, calling all Shakers "wolves in sheep's clothing, sniffing the prey from afar, come to rend and devour."

John Thompson also denounced the easterners, charging that "the false prophets and liars were parting man and wife, breaking up families and churches, and taking away people's lands."

In spite of this opposition, the first western society was formed at Turtle Creek, Ohio. On May 23, 1805, forty Believers "for the first time in the Miami or Western Country, went forth in the worship of God in the dance." A few weeks later on July 29 three additional eastern leaders—David Darrow, Daniel Moseley, and Solomon King—arrived from New Lebanon. With Darrow duly appointed the official leader of the Western Church and with two other strong back-up men, the three original Shaker messengers were freed to extend their missionary efforts throughout the rest of Ohio and Indiana and to follow up the work they had already started in Kentucky.

The trips were not easy. There were times in Indiana and Ohio when there would be no cabin for a distance of 150 miles. Such desolation increased the dangers the men encountered from Indians and wild animals. The travelers had to cross streams and rivers by wading or fording, by swimming, or by riding chance logs that floated by. Bates wrote that swollen streams, along with snow banks and icestorms, were among the many hazards of winter travel. On one journey both of Bates's big toe nails were destroyed by frostbite. On another he suffered from frozen "footens" or socks and from shoes that were too small.

Usually the men traveled in twos or threes with one or two

new converts accompanying one of the veterans. The crossing into Kentucky from Ohio was made either at Cincinnati or at Limestone, later to be called Maysville. During 1805–1806 the Kentucky visits were usually made in Washington and Flemingsburg, Concord, Cane Ridge and Paris, Danville and Lexington, Long Lick, Shawnee Run, Paint Lick, and settlements in Shelby County.

On Friday, August 16, 1805, when Benjamin Youngs, Richard McNemar, and Malcolm Worley were near Danville, three Mercer County men—Elisha Thomas and Samuel and John Banta—came and asked them to come to a private house and give their testimony. Shortly afterward Elisha "opened his mind," thus becoming the first Kentucky convert. The Shakers made regular visits to central Kentucky, but it was not until the following January that Benjamin and Richard McNemar heard the second and third confessions in Kentucky—those of James Dickson and his wife.

Although large crowds gathered for the Shaker meetings, the brethren felt that most of the people came principally out of curiosity to see the converts "labor or march their songs." But curiosity and indifference could be tolerated better than the violence that occurred at times. For example, in November 1805, while they were in Danville, the Shakers found that the enemy had cut off the ears and tails of the Shaker horses.

But by early 1806 there was a growing number of the Shawnee Run and Paint Lick converts. Among these were members of the Banta, Shields, Thomas, Vibbard, Maxwell, Sasseen, and Dean families. Also accepting the Shaker doctrines were the Presbyterian minister Matthew Houston and his wife Peggy; Charles Rikirs and his wife Polly; Isaac Newton and his servant, a bright mulatto, part Indian; the widow Tiny Verbreke; John Woods, a young preacher; J. Biggers; Henry Hutton; and Samuel Harris.

Interest in Shakerism continued to grow and crowds increased. Once 300 people assembled in John Banta's barn; 800 gathered in the barn of Elisha Thomas, and upwards of 1,000 at Samuel Banta's barn. Various members of the crowd would be "exercised in dancing" and the Believers would continue singing and dancing till near day.

Between meetings the Shaker leaders would visit in the homes of the scattered converts, counseling them and warning them about "opening their minds in disorder," that is, embracing false doctrines. The deportment of the young Kentucky Believers was noted favorably by some of their neighbors. The Tobias Wilhite family entertained two Shaker brothers who had come to the Wilhites to buy salt. The fact that the Shakers knelt in prayer before and after each meal impressed the Wilhites to the extent that both Tobias and his wife as well as several of their twelve grown children accepted the Shaker tenets.

Back in Ohio there was rejoicing that ten more New Lebanon recruits, four brethren and six sisters, had arrived on May 31, 1806. Several of these easterners, Samuel Turner, Molly Goodrich, and Peter Pease, would later become the appointed leaders for the new Kentucky societies.

In the meantime some of the Shawnee Run converts were appointed by Elder Benjamin to assume certain responsibilities. Elisha Thomas was "to stand first in our absence, Isaac Dean to take charge of the farm, and Cornelius Banta and Joe Shields to work in the joiner shop." The Believers who had been living scattered throughout the area began moving to Shawnee Run, and the little community started to take shape on Elder Thomas's 140-acre holdings, which lay on both sides of Shawnee Run.

In November 1806 thirteen of the Shawnee Run society made their first trip to Union Village, Ohio, traveling on horseback and in a four-horse wagon. Making the trip were Elisha, Polly, and Sally Thomas, Polly and Sally Shields, Samuel, Henry, and Rachael Banta, Matthew Houston, Anne Bruner, Peggy Biggers, Nancy Harris, and William Gordon. As a present they carried "100 pounds of tobacco, 20 gallons of boiled cider, 8 bushels of dried apples, some dried gummer grapes, and 12 pounds of butter, also some cotton and wool and sweet potatoes."

During the seventeen-day visit in Ohio two significant

events took place. On November 16 at an evening meeting Elder Benjamin washed the Kentucky brethren's feet. The gesture was returned on the evening of the twenty-first when Henry Banta

after much entreaty had the privilege of satisfying his feelings to kiss the feet of all the brethren who came from New Lebanon. Accordingly while they were sitting in a rank eight in number, he began with Benjamin and Issachar and went through pulling off their shoes and kissing all their feet—William Gordon also followed and then Henry returned and repeated the operation putting on their shoes again. Then they renewed the meeting in songs and dances, strong, powerful, and comfortable.

While the Shawnee Run Believers were at Union Village, Elder Benjamin began writing a covenant for the emerging society. Armed with this new covenant, the Kentuckians "set out for home—truly under a blessing and much union and love visibly manifested."

Later in the society's church record, B. B. Dunlavy wrote of their return trip: "At sunset they crossed the Ohio river at Cincinnati and put up at Kennedy's, where in the evening they met in an upper chamber and went forth in the worship. Their singing was plainly heard on the streets of Cincinnati on the opposite side of the river by Elder Peter Pease."

Dunlavy went on to praise the pioneer society members, saying: "Nothing appear'd too hard for them to do for the gospel's sake. The sisters particularly were nearly all in perfect uniform in the order of Believers from head to foot, neat, clean, and exemplary as if they had had a privilege for years."

On December 3, 1806, immediately after the group arrived home, forty-four members of the Shawnee Run society entered into the newly written covenant "dedicating themselves and all their property to the material benefit of each other."

In June 1807, the Union Village ministry paid their first official visit to the new Shawnee Run society. The ministry, Elder David Darrow and Eldress Ruth Farrington, were accompanied by Daniel Moseley, Solomon King, Molly Goodrich, and Ruth Darrow.

Now that the Mercer County society had been organized, the eastern leaders began to think of pushing on to the Gasper River territory, the original seat of the Great Revival in Kentucky.

By October 15 Bates, accompanied by the new converts Richard McNemar and Matthew Houston, was on his way, going through Bullitt County "southward to Elizabethtown, Bacon Creek, Green river, Mammoth Cave, Dripping Springs, and across Barren river into Warren County." On Saturday the seventeenth they arrived at the home of John Rankin, minister of the Gasper River Presbyterian congregation, and were "received with a measure of kindness."

The next day Rankin took Matthew Houston with him to an appointment at Mud River. The other two went to the Gasper meetinghouse, but were forbidden to speak. It was then that John Sloss invited them to come six miles west to his house and preach to the people who wanted to hear them. On Tuesday the three Believers went twenty-five miles to the home of George Walls on Drakes Creek where they were "kindly received" and where they preached. Returning to John Rankin's house, the three began visiting throughout the Gasper neighborhood and became acquainted with the families of Charles Eads, Jess McComb, Samuel Robinson, and one Porter.

On the Sabbath, October 25, a number collected at Samuel Robinson's to hear the word, and at a Monday meeting at Gasper, "the people agreed that we should speak." On Tuesday an appointment was given to preach at John Shannon's. Here the Shakers heard their first confession—that of John McComb of Red Banks, who was visiting his daughter Sally. Two days later Jess McComb, Neal Patterson, and John Rankin, the Gasper minister, all "opened their minds," to be followed next day by Charles Eads and his wife.

The first Sabbath in November the three visitors preached in the Gasper meetinghouse. During the remaining part of their month's visit, the men heard twenty other confessions, making twenty-six Believers at Gasper. Two of these were slaves—Neptune, belonging to Francis Whyte, and Betty Freehart, a yellow woman.

Within a month after his first visit, Issachar Bates returned to Gasper from Ohio. This time he was accompanied by John Dunlavy and Matthew Houston.

Although the great thrust of their visit was at Gasper, Bates did go some miles distant to Red River and there "garnered a number of proselytes," who became some of the most substantial members at Gasper. Among these were Thomas McLean and Mary, his wife; her brother Robert Paisley; William Johns and his wife; and Absalom Chisholm with two adopted daughters, Keturah and Peninah Harrison.

Other trips took the brethren to speak in a schoolhouse in Hartford, at the courthouse in Madisonville, and at Red Banks, to be known later as Paducah.

Until the society could be formally organized under the direction of an official ministry, John Rankin and Jess McComb were the natural leaders, for it was in their homes and in some adjoining cabins that the members first took residence.

As time passed, the Shaker venture in Ohio and Kentucky continued to develop. A first-hand description of the two westernmost societies was written at Shawnee Run in December 1807, and sent on its way to Mother Lucy Wright, head of the New Lebanon ministry.

She must have read with interest that the Pleasant Hill members

live in a thick settled place of Kentucky, is in the center of the inhabited part of the country west of the Allegheny mountains and south of Canada. Having the state of Ohio on the north and Tennessee on the south, the country we live in is in the center of the state, the central point is about four miles distant from us. This state contains a great deal of very beautiful land level and rich, some of which has borders very close upon us. The spot where we live is not quite so even as we could wish, yet it is not mountainous like New Lebanon. There is no mountain in sight and the soil is rich and fertile. We are situated on a river by the name of Kentucky river which a considerable part of the year is navigable for boats for about one hundred and forty or fifty miles from its mouth where it empties into the Ohio. The Believers' land is bounded by it on the east, our house stands about three quarters of a mile from it. Up this river there is a number of inexhaustible banks of stone coal, the same with sea coal, which they bring down in boats for blacksmithing and other uses.

Doubtless it was with equal interest and pleasure that Mother Lucy read: "The Believers in Gasper river have as level and beautiful habitation as almost any to be found in the world. This place is almost an hundred and thirty miles from here. We have been three journeys there this season. They generally keep the faith and increase a little in number."

A few years later Molly Goodrich, then a Gasper eldress, also sent a description of her home to New Lebanon: "The more this place is improved, the better we like it. The land is level and handsome, and wonderful springs of good water and streams large enough to carry mills and any kind of water power. The timber in this land is scarce. Therefore the brethren have bargained for a piece of land, well timbered, about four miles off on the Black Lick Creek."

Having gathered together on good lands in Mercer and Logan counties, the Kentucky Shakers were ready to carry through their communal experiment.

2

PUTTING THEIR
HANDS TO WORK

ABOUT TWO YEARS after the Shawnee Run and Gasper societies "gathered" on the land belonging to one or more early converts, an official ministry for each was recommended by the Union Village ministry and approved by the New Lebanon parent ministry.

Beginning in January 1809, John Meacham, Samuel Turner, Lucy Smith, and Anna Cole composed the Shawnee Run ministry. In September 1811, Benjamin Seth Youngs, Joseph Allen, Molly Goodrich, and Mercy Pickett were established at Gasper.

That the easterners, experienced in the Shaker life, were welcomed is seen in an 1810 letter sent to New Lebanon by Eldress Lucy, who wrote:

More than a year before we came, Elisha Thomas had offered Elder John a horse, saddle, and bridle with spending money, etc.—to go where and when he would if he would come to live in Shawneetown. For some time before we moved, Elder John and some others of us visited Kentucky quite often and their feelings immediately increased for us to come to stay with them. . . . At length Elder John told them if they would build a place to live, we would some of us come.

Having been promised support, the new ministry arrived bringing only fifty dollars, two beds and bedding, and a few smaller things. A new log house was ready for them.

Soon after the two ministries began effecting the essential organization, the name of each society was changed—Shawnee Run to Pleasant Hill, Gasper to South Union. Another early action was to appoint trustees whose responsibilities were to initiate and conduct the society business with "the world." Later as memberships grew, the ministries appointed elders and eldresses to direct the affairs of the family groups. Also official society journals were begun by the head elder in each ministry.

With all the pressing needs, it must have been difficult for the ministries to set priorities. Should they begin to build the essential shops and dwellings, buy lands needed for future farming operations, search for necessary supplies to begin various industries, help the trustees establish trading relationships, or instruct and further organize the young Believers? How much time should they spend in further recruiting throughout the area?

To meet such a challenge required strong leadership and a dedication to the Shaker cause. The ministries, each headed by one of the original eastern missionaries, were equal to the challenge. They put their own hands to work and expected all others to do the same.

To increase their land holdings, the Pleasant Hill trustees bought adjoining acreage that could be turned into more fields and orchards. The South Union trustees also bought some neighboring land, but they looked for "timbered" lands and land with streams to supplement their water power even though such land proved to be some distance from their settlement. Usually the land was purchased by means of a down payment and a promise of three yearly payments. It was expected that the essential funds would accrue from the sale of lands belonging to future members.

Since most of the land purchased by the society had never been cultivated, it had to be "grubbed" before crops could be planted and orchards could be set. The society journals reflect the long hours spent in preparing the new lands for cultivation.

From the daily records one learns how "the brethren finished grubbing a new society field of 32 acres," and how thirty-six schoolboys began to clear it off and burn the brush. A few days later the brethren commenced cleaning ten more acres, and on succeeding March days, "all hands great and small, aged, middleaged, and youth" worked in the new meadow ground.

The buying of land continued over a long period of years. As late as 1864 Pleasant Hill purchased some additional land, the object being to obtain control of the ferry: "January 4. Purchased ⅝ of a tract of land on cliff bordering on the Kentucky river on the east side opposite the mouth of Dix river and Cedar Run including the ferry on that side—this side of the ferry being previously in our possession. The whole tract contains about 130 acres—the greater portion of which is cliffs. The ⅝ part cost $3,200."

The Pleasant Hill land holdings reached approximately 7,000 acres, whereas those of South Union totaled 6,000 acres. By the 1870s the Pleasant Hill holdings had been cut to 4,200 acres. At the time of the South Union sale in 1922 that society had consolidated its lands into one home farm of 4,133 acres.

The building program in each village was launched early, and it continued far into the century with Pleasant Hill building a frame storehouse as late as 1870 and additional brick smokehouses in 1875 and 1889. South Union built a large brick hotel in 1869, a steam flour mill in 1870, and a new dwelling house for the West family as late as 1883. Also a wooden store building was replaced with a brick one in 1896. The total number of buildings constructed at Pleasant Hill is listed as 266. The number at South Union was also relatively high.

To read the early Pleasant Hill records is to realize how much time and effort were required for the society's building program. "December 28, 1808 Building. In this year the first sawmill was built at Shawnee Run."

But that sawmill had to be rebuilt twice, first in 1809 after the dam was carried away by a flood and again in 1812 after the mill was burned by incendiaries.

In March 1809, the brethren built a "meeting house or rather a shed with the floor of Mother earth" which served not only as the first constructed place of worship but as temporary housing for four new families. Another family had to be lodged at the tannery, creating an urgent need to provide better housing before winter.

So early in June the brethren began constructing a stone dwelling to replace the earlier log dwelling of the Church family and to provide housing for those who were in temporary quarters. The ministry thought it prudent to build with stone because they had a number of quarries of high quality.

By December 19 it could be reported that the Church family under the care of James Gass and Betsy Banta had moved into their new dwelling house and that they ate in their new kitchen for the first time at breakfast the day before Christmas, when thirty-six sat down at one time.

The two-story house, 30 by 24 feet, with a cellar under the whole of it, was described as being done in a "plain modest stile" with the inside wood painted a stone color, the same as used in New Lebanon. The people who lived in the house were reported to be "equally as beautiful as their house. . . . However, the nearby dependencies continued to be built of logs. Among these were the kitchen, a stable for the horses and cattle, and a double shop with a double stone chimney between."

Also built in 1809 was a log schoolhouse, located about one-half mile northwest of the church.

The next year brought a continuation of the steady building program. Given priority was a proper meetinghouse to replace the 1809 shed. Built of stone, the 55-by-45–foot meetinghouse contained living quarters for the ministry. When completed, the new quarters were "done off neat and very convenient." The interior of the church was painted blue.

Ten years later a frame meetinghouse, 60 by 44 feet, was begun to replace the 1810 stone one, which was "not so much in the center as the Believers wished" and which had been somewhat cracked by one of the New Madrid earthquakes. Elder Samuel Turner described the new church: "A very strong substantial frame it is and neatly finished off both outside and in. . . . we moved into the meeting house 14th of November and had our first meeting on the 19th and we found it not any too large for all who attended the first meeting to labor at one time."

This 1820 Pleasant Hill meetinghouse remains today as a standing memorial to the architectural skill and ingenuity of the Shaker builders.

The South Union leaders, too, felt the need to replace their first small meetinghouse. Late in 1813 the brethren began digging the foundation, hauling the timbers and stone, and firing brick kilns. The fact that most of the South Union buildings were being constructed of brick was explained to the eastern ministry by Elder Benjamin. "We are much put to it for a little building timber as it is extremely scarce here. What little there is, hard to get at and very dear by the time we get it, but building stone of different kinds and the best kind of materials for brick we have convenient and in plenty."

Because of the press of other work, such as developing the newly acquired Drakes Creek mill property, it was not until the summer of 1817 that the first course of "blue stone" was laid and the first story of the South Union meetinghouse was raised with block and tackle. The walls were completed and the 66-by-46–foot house roofed by October 1818.

The next April four brethren from Union Village and three from Pleasant Hill came "to assist in finishing the meetinghouse" and stayed until the joiner work was completed. Although much remained to be done, it was decided to hold a dedicatory service on the Sunday before the visiting workmen were to leave. Elder Benjamin thought the day was "all pleasant as a May morning."

Earlier the same year, January 17, 1819, "President James Monroe and suit, Gen'l Jackson and family" stopped at South Union. No doubt Elder Benjamin pointed out the handsome exterior of the new meetinghouse and invited the noted visitors to stop again when they could attend services in the new church.

By the end of the next summer the interior had been plastered and painted. When the stone hearths had been laid in the ministry's upper living quarters, the building was declared finished.

So on October 1, 1820, "at ½ past eight o'clock in the evening" the South Union society met for the first service in the completed brick meetinghouse. Only one month later, the Pleasant Hill society was to occupy its new frame church.

Unfortunately the South Union meetinghouse no longer stands. It was razed in the 1920s to be replaced with a modern residence made of the original bricks.

Second only in importance to the Shaker meetinghouses were the Church family or Centre House dwellings. Again earlier Church dwellings were to be replaced with larger ones. In each community the new Centre building would stand directly across from the society meetinghouse.

In the early 1820s when the two societies began to construct their unusually large buildings, Kentucky was still a relatively young state and the societies' neighboring towns of Bowling Green and Russellville, Lexington and Harrodsburg were small towns largely surrounded by uncultivated land.

Yet the Mercer County Shakers planned and constructed a limestone building measuring 60 by 55 feet with a 34-by-85–foot L or T, making the whole length 140 feet. Their sister society in more sparsely settled Logan County built a brick and stone structure which was 61 by 48½ feet with a T and a stairway annex bringing the entire length to 142 feet. In those days passersby in wagons or on horseback must have been startled to come upon the large Georgian houses dominating the rural Kentucky landscape.

It is not possible to calculate the number of man-hours spent in quarrying and dressing the great limestone blocks, in firing the brick, and in cutting and hauling the timber needed in the construction of the two Centre houses. But to view these buildings today is to realize that the early Shakers had to be motivated far beyond the ordinary desire to provide a dwelling.

Not only time but skill and physical strength were demanded. The Pleasant Hill brethren found that raising their loft timbers was a "powerful heavy job," and certainly the South Union men who raised the long, solid-limestone eave troughs onto their Church Family House must have found the work demanding.

With such durable features as copper-lined gutters and a stone foundation 9 feet 8 inches high and 28 inches thick, it is understandable that Elder Benjamin thought the forty-room South Union Centre House "would stand a thousand years unless it was shaken down by an earthquake or something of that kind."

Over the years the visiting Shakers from the East usually referred in their travel journals to the "great" houses. It was Anna White who wrote the New Lebanon kitchen sisters describing the South Union Centre House as being "very high between lofts so that you need an elevator to carry you from kitchen to attic." Today anyone who climbs the fifty-seven steps in the three original flights of stairs will be inclined to agree.

Work on the buildings was not constant. Instead construction advanced as time and materials were available. A letter written in August 1826 from Pleasant Hill to the New Lebanon ministry explained that the new Centre House was covered and that soon the building would be "pointed down, the glass put in, and the window shutters and doors hung and painted. It will look as good as it ever will—so we will not do much more at it for a little while as the brethren are pretty crowded with other business."

At both colonies part of the other business was preparing to build the rest of the major permanent houses—that is, the trustees' office, the ministry's house, and the dwellings for the remaining East, West, and North families. To the Shakers a *family* was a group or class of members. For example, the Church or Senior family, which occupied the Centre House, was composed of all members who had signed the covenant; whereas, the East or Gathering family consisted of those newcomers who were still being taught what it was like to be a Shaker. Some would stay to join; some would leave.

To construct more buildings was to need more supplies. So at both societies there was a constant "readying" of the essential timber, stone, and brick. Also trips had to be made to Nashville and Louisville, Cincinnati and Pittsburgh, to obtain glass, iron hardware, and other items that were not being produced at home. On occasion arrangements had to be made at city banks to obtain short-term loans needed to meet obligations for both land purchases and construction costs.

Around each family dwelling house were clustered numerous small dependencies, such as the butter house, the fruit-drying house, the chickenhouse, the woodshed, the round bee house, and the silk house. Other functional structures were the garden tool house, the wagon shed, the carriage house, the machine shop, the slaughterhouse, the smokehouse, and the lime shed, as well as shops for working with seeds, brooms, and straw hats, shops for the wheelwright and the carpenter, the tailor and the shoemaker, the cooper and the blacksmith.

Each family also needed a horse- and cow-barn, an ox stable, grain barns, and the corncribs. Icehouses were built. Also the sisters in each family were provided with "necessaries" or backhouses, some of them 16 feet long. For the men there would be a wash- or bathhouse.

The community mills and the tanyard were built along a waterway, at some distance from the village center. Each society soon was operating a gristmill, a fulling mill, and a sawmill. Pleasant Hill had an early linseed oil mill, and both societies established woolen mills. For a few years South Union had a whiskey distillery.

As time went on, some of the early buildings were razed and others were moved and converted to new functions. At Pleasant Hill "the old frame house where Samuel Banta collected a family in 1807" was pulled down and moved to clear a site for the new North Lot family buildings. South Union found it expedient to take down Jess McComb's old brick house, the first building occupied by Believers when they gathered on Gasper River.

When any building was moved, great care was exercised. A journal entry reads: "We took off the roof in 4 pieces—took down all the logs and took up the floor whole. Raised the building and finished it off as far as the body and roof is concerned." Thus an old crib was moved to serve as a temporary washhouse at the new South Union Centre House.

Not only the buildings, but the grounds also required attention. Stone walks had to be laid, fences had to be built and kept in good repair. The first step in building a picket fence around the South Union Centre House was to bury a short stone base or foot on which to set each cedar post. Here indeed is evidence that Mother Ann's western children heeded their leader's early admonition to do all their work as if they had a thousand years to live.

In 1835 a Pleasant Hill elder reported to the New Lebanon ministry: "Our buildings are in good repair so our employ this year will be erecting good fences around and about our buildings as well as out on the plantation and leveling and smoothing of our dooryards also. All of which you know we ought to pay as respect to its proper time and season so that we may not be a reproach to the cause in our going forth in this place."

Evidently the leveling was effective, for when Frances Murrell of New Lebanon was visiting Pleasant Hill in August 1847, she wrote in her journal: "This place has been so much improved since I saw it 23 years ago that I should hardly have known it. They have filled up the hollows with the hills which made it appear quite level about their buildings."

Frances also admired the new stone fencing and learned that the brothers intended to "keep on building stone fence . . . until their whole premises are enclosed."

Another accomplishment that pleased Frances was the piping of water into all four of the large family dwellings. During her visit she inquired about the project and learned that it had been begun in September 1831 under the direction of Micajah Burnett and had been completed in the Church family on

April 30, 1833. The entire project had reached completion in 1838. Frances was pleased to learn that the Mercer County Shakers were the first Kentuckians to have installed a water system and furthermore theirs was only the second system west of the Alleghenies.

Much of the correspondence sent out of Pleasant Hill in the early 1830s carried detailed descriptions of the exciting new water project. On September 12, 1832, John R. Bryant wrote a letter to Brother Stephen Munson in the East:

Our exertion this season to supply the village with water by mechanical power has so far been prosperous. At the fountain north of the village we sunk a pool in the solid rock 9 ft. deep averaging 11 × 13 feet diameter, which is supplemented by 2 small but never failing streams of pure water which is secured above ground with good walls and a suitable frame and roof.

The force pumps with all their apparatus are completed and thus far they perform beyond our most sanguine expectations.

After the water had been supplied to the Church family, Samuel Turner wrote to New Lebanon further expressing the society leaders' confidence that the "water conveyance" system would meet with success.

Samuel explained that by means of a force pump, a two-inch column of water was raised 125 feet and was then forced uphill to "its place of deposit" through 600 yards of cast-iron pipe, secured at the joints with lead. It could from there be drawn down to every kitchen, washhouse, and cellar in the Church family, "where we have nothing to do but turn a key and draw the best of water. . . . our tanners who attend to it have nothing to do but hitch the horse to the shaft and start him."

Reflecting the Shaker consideration for their animals, Samuel continued by commenting that "without any detriment to the horse, they can force up water enough in one hour to supply the Church."

One of the last steps was to construct a 22-by-15–foot two-story frame building over the cistern for the purpose of "keeping the water cool in the summer and from freezing in the winter."

By the spring of 1837 the South Union trustees were corresponding with Micajah about the installation of their own water system. During the summer they gathered together the recommended supplies in anticipation of his arrival in October, when he was "to take the oversight, direction, and management of the business relating to our contemplated water works according to a previous arrangement between Pleasant Hill and South Union."

It was found that the North House spring or well would be a dependable supply. The well was paved or lined with stones to a height of about twenty feet and stairs were built down into the well which was "some 10 to 12 feet in diameter." By means of horse power, the water was pumped through "cast metal aqueducts," into a cistern about 100 rods away. An earthen mound braced the walls of the circular cistern which measured 9 feet in depth and 13 feet across. The cistern wall was made of brick, plastered inside with hydraulic cement. The bottom of the cistern was described as being two feet above the natural surface of the ground.

From the cistern, the water was conveyed by gravity flow through lead pipes to "all the kitchens, wash houses, and stables" that pertained to the first and second families, including the West House. The North family received water from "branches that lead off the main aqueducts."

Micajah's helpful visit to South Union was not an exceptional one, for it was customary for the Shaker leaders to exchange both ideas and actual labor in large undertakings. On January 23, 1846, Jacob Voris wrote to South Union saying that Pleasant Hill was considering building a new wash mill. He asked: "Are you pleased with yours now as you were last summer? Or has time and experience shown need of alteration? We need dimensions of your mill, length of the draft arm and length of the crank. . . . Also did you leave the pattern of your castings in Louisville? If so, can we have them?"

And so the villages took form. Not only did visitors admire the carefully planned and constructed Kentucky Shakertowns, but members themselves felt proud of what had been accomplished. In a letter published in the *Shaker*, Hortency G.

Hooser of Pleasant Hill spoke of the architectural heritage left by the earlier society members:

I have watched the rise and progress of Pleasant Hill from my child-hood up for sixty-two years. I saw the brethren with their own indus-trious hands fell the sturdy oaks and maples, right there where our large and commodious dwellings now stand and have stood for very long years. I saw very soon, young as I was, that they sought first the kingdom of heaven and then by giving hearts to God and putting their hands to work, they wrought wonders in this land.

Nancy Rupe also expressed appreciation of the Pleasant Hill founders in an eighteen-stanza poem. One verse read:

You came to this spot a wilderness drear
With a living faith and a godly fear.
Thus by his power did persevere
And reared this Pleasant Hill.

During the years the neat and well-ordered villages were developing, the surrounding lands were being turned into well-defined garden plots, orchards, pasture lands, and tilled fields.

The Shaker fields were first planted with crops that would meet immediate needs—wheat, corn, rye, oats, flax, and hemp. A South Union journal entry in June 1814 reflects the satisfaction felt when "100 acres of good wheat were divided among 300 people." The elder wrote that it would seem that there could not be much complaint with one-third of an acre of good wheat for each person, besides one-half acre of corn per head. Two summers later the South Union wheat crop of 128 acres was cut by "21 brethren, 20 youths, 7 black brethren, and 3 hirelings." It was estimated that "one good hand with sickle reaps two acres a day."

The 1833 Pleasant Hill ministerial report to New Lebanon stated: "We have between 2,000 and 3,000 acres of wheat, rye and oats. Besides our flax and 100 acres of Indian corn, broom corn, and potatoes. So upon the whole we have business enough to keep us busy in doing good and no time to spare in vain amusement or working mischief."

Although vain amusements were not tolerated, the Shaker leaders did understand the need for occasional lightening of the heavy work program with fun and a competitive spirit, and so grubbing bees, logrollings, and chopping frolics were arranged for the men and boys, spinning frolics and other bees for the sisters.

When corn-gathering time came in the late fall, the Kentucky Shakers followed the folk custom of having a corn husking, usually on a moonlit night. Two captains would choose sides, a signal would be given, and then the huskers would begin "on a long ridge of corn," tossing the husked ears into two separate piles. The onlookers cheered and encouraged the huskers. When the winning side had been declared, all joined in eating roast pig and drinking coffee or sassafras tea.

Such contests not only satisfied a desire for fun but they undoubtedly increased the production. For example, two young Shaker brothers entered a race to determine who could plait the most hat straw in a day. During sixteen hours of actual work, one braided 120 yards of straw, the other 114 yards. But the winner declared the race a draw, saying, "Milton's was as much better as mine was longer." Normally it was thought that if a man braided two hundred yards in a month, along with his other tasks, he had done remarkably well.

Crops other than grain were added to the Shaker economy, some of them experimental. In 1857 South Union was trying a new cane. "Chinese Sugar Cane. This cane lately introduced into this country called Sorgho and another called Imphur seems to flourish north of us. . . . we have concluded to try the Sorgho and see if we cannot obtain molasses at least better and cheaper than we usually get south from Louisiana cane." Pleasant Hill also was trying the Chinese cane, with the East family making 178 gallons of molasses in October 1858. The grinding was done on a new cast-iron mill bought for that purpose.

After reading an ad in the *American Bee Journal*, Elder Benjamin Dunlavy of Pleasant Hill decided to try a new clover he saw advertised. By the 1860s the societies were raising sweet potatoes for sale at $2.00 per bushel. In the spring there were potato slips for sale. In May 1862, the South Union Society set out 13,800 hills, putting "two quarts of water in each hill." Once an unexpected killing frost early in the autumn sent the South Union sisters out to help the brethren dig twenty-two acres of potatoes.

There were crop failures in the Shaker fields as well as elsewhere, because of periods of drought, ravages of the Hessian fly, army worms in the meadow, rust in the wheat, or perhaps a lack of the snow needed by spring wheat.

The Pleasant Hill wheat crop of 1830 was the "heaviest ever," but the 2,500 bushels had to be threshed quickly because of the weevil. Elder Samuel Turner wrote, "If the wheat is got out right after harvest and put into the cellar where it will be kept cool, it will prevent the ravages of the weevil." A weevil-infested wheat crop three years later was being kiln-dried, which caused "a considerable increase of labor."

Since the production of wheat was so vital to the well-being of the societies, a crop failure was always recorded in the journal accounts and explained in the annual ministerial reports to the Mother Society in New Lebanon. In 1865 there was no wheat to ship from central Kentucky. "The average yield was not over a fourth of a crop . . . our own included, tho it was among the best, but it makes poor flour."

All Shaker societies had extensive fruit orchards, with 400 to 800 trees set out at one time. The first orchards were replaced regularly with new stock, and from time to time additional orchards were started. A regular program of grafting was maintained. Large strawberry patches and well-tended vineyards were also to be seen on Shaker lands.

Those charged with overseeing the fruit had to be alert. An unusually late spring frost meant kindling fires in the peach orchards; an unusually dry spring called for watering the strawberry plants from barrels set on wheels.

True to their habit of experimenting, the Shakers planted and tested many new varieties of fruit. A letter dated November 9, 1857, from Brother Urban of South Union to Brother Giles Avery of New Lebanon mentioned that the muscadine grapevines received as a gift two years earlier had borne "delicious fruit" and had proved "more hardy and less liable to rot and mildew than the Catawba or Isobella." Therefore the Kentucky Shakers believed it would prove to be a fine wine grape.

Urban also wrote that he had recently discussed the muscadine with the "large winemaker Nicholas Longworth of Cincinnati," who condemned the northern grape although he had never tried it. Urban said, "We think he is mistaken." Certainly the Shaker mind would have condemned the refusal to experiment.

The orchards were a source not only of pride and profit, but also of aesthetic pleasure. One Pleasant Hill journalist wrote: "The pear, peach, plum, and cherry trees and even the little barberry bush are in bloom. The scene is most delightful!" A South Union scribe found pleasure in all "the fruit trees along the creek shining green."

Every harvest season meant a busy time of gathering and processing. The season began with the ripening of the strawberries and May cherries and ended with the wild grapes and late fall apples. So for a large part of the year fresh fruit was available for making pies, cobblers, and sauces as well as for drying, canning, and preserving. Cider, wines, and cordials were also made and stored in the cellar rooms, some to be used for medicinal purposes at home and the rest to be sold to the world.

In the 1830s when the fruit crops began to exceed home needs, the surplus products were placed on the market. This expansion meant the building of drying houses and preserving houses in order to free the kitchens for meal preparation. By the 1870s and 1880s the sale of the canned and preserved fruit proved to be the principal source of income for each Kentucky society. The glass jars, each containing four pounds of preserves, were packed twelve to a wooden case.

To meet the market demands, the trustees began to buy supplementary fruit. When an unfavorable season cut the society crops, efforts were doubled to find sufficient outside supplies. Pleasant Hill trustees bought from their Mercer and Boyle county neighbors as well as farther afield in Laurel and

Rockcastle counties, and they even ordered fruit sent "on the railroad cars from Indiana." The South Union trustees also contracted fruit from outside sources. Often fruit was bought in Louisville and shipped by rail to the society.

Some of the sisters and children, accompanied by a driver, would go to pick the fruit that had been engaged in the area. Once while gathering wild grapes, a brother and six sisters were caught in a heavy rainstorm. Another time a brother got a painful sunburn on his bald head. He was admonished to cover his head with a damp cloth at future pickings.

One needs only to read the society records to comprehend the extent of the fruit industry. For example, the South Union Church family account for May 1872 shows that beginning on the twenty-second the women made 3,501 quarts of cherry and strawberry preserves in a ten-day period. Even on Sunday the twenty-sixth the women put up 231 jars and attended one meeting. June did not bring an end to the work, for on the next Sabbath, June 2, the sisters finished 155 quarts of cherry preserves and attended two meetings. The same week some of the brethren took 212 pounds of honey.

At Pleasant Hill the three-year total for 1858–1860 was 55,115 jars of processed fruit. No wonder one reads that "the brethren unite with the sisters in the preserve manufacturing," or that "we put off washing and all hands turned out and gathered strawberries for preserves." The children helped not only by picking some of the fruit but by "gathering chips for the preserve making."

A letter from Eldress Nancy E. Moore of South Union to Elder O. C. Hamilton of Union Village, Ohio, explained that successful preserve making resulted from "having plenty of water put in at first so that the fruit may not thicken before it is thoroughly cooked." She explained further that "when the children gather half ripe strawberries, we don't like to lose them, so we separate the green from the ripe fruit and cook each to themselves . . . and after they are well cooked, we pour them into large bowls and mix them together to cook." Sometimes they scalded the unripened fruit and pressed the juice to use in cooking the ripe fruit.

In 1874 a friend placed some jars of South Union preserves on exhibit in the Mechanic and Agricultural Exposition of Louisiana "where they were awarded a diploma for the best preserves put up in glass in the United States."

Preserving and canning were supplemented by the making of jellies and apple butter and by the cutting and drying of the peaches and the apples. Also prepared for sale as well as for home use were tomato preserves, cucumber pickles, and at Pleasant Hill "Ice Melons."

The preserving industry was only one of the many ways the sisters put their hands to work. Each day brought its quota of routine tasks such as cooking and cleaning, washing and ironing, weaving and sewing. The 1848 annual report from Pleasant Hill shows some of the contributions the women made to the society needs. Listed among the year's weaving and sewing were 90 yards of towel linen, 52 of fine flannel, and 52 of underbedding. Also there were 28 yards of "all worsted" and 34 gray handkerchiefs. Reported too were 36 drab cloaks, 63 linsey gowns, 42 pair of men's trousers, 32 shirts, 12 jackets, and 20 hats.

To read the accounts kept at both societies is to understand how versatile the sisters were in their weaving. From their looms came cheesecloth, wool sheets, carpet runners, and druggets, as well as chair tapes or "listing," cap tape, and straw bordering for bonnets.

Somehow the sisters found time for other work such as making cheese, soap by the barrel, and candles by the gross. Before the time of kerosene lamps, candles were needed not only for the dwelling houses but also for the numerous shops and mills.

The sisters also did outside work. In the spring they helped drop the corn seed; in the fall they joined in the husking. Later they gathered up the husks to be used in making mattresses and in bottoming chairs. They helped to gather all the garden and field seeds raised for the market, to worm the peach trees, to pick up wood chips, and to cut the straw needed in making bonnets and hats. They did the milking, picked the dried beans, and later sorted them. They pulled weeds from the church walk, and once the South Union women held a road-repairing bee.

Sometimes it fell to the kitchen sisters "to prepare a nice dinner and send it out to the workers," who were too far away to come home for the meal. On occasion they had to conduct the daily service while the men completed some demanding task. During seasonal work, such as timber cutting, at one of the out farms, several sisters would go along to do the cooking.

The most unusual work carried on by the Kentucky sisters was that of the silk industry, which existed primarily between 1825 and 1875. Each society had its row of mulberry trees. Children helped the sisters in pulling the leaves and placing them in the worm trays. Care had to be taken that wet leaves were never used. Later they helped in carrying the large baskets of cocoons to the tubs of boiling water. But the tedious work of unwinding the cocoon fiber was left to the skillful fingers of the sisters.

The Pleasant Hill records contain numerous references to the silk industry. One learns that on certain days the sisters commenced "spooling the white silk for handkerchiefs," finished "warping a silk piece," or "beamed the said piece of silk." In 1854 the Pleasant Hill brethren were putting out more mulberry trees.

However the silk industry at South Union seems to have been larger than at Pleasant Hill. Pride in the sisters' manufacture was often expressed in the South Union journals.

Jan. 1, 1832. <u>Silk Domestic</u>. The sisters all appeared dressed in their homemade silk kerchiefs the first time at South Union.

Jan. 1, 1833. <u>Sisters' New Year's Present to the Brethren</u>. As soon as we rose from our supper we repaired to the meeting room to receive a New Year's gift from the good sisters, consisting of a beautiful silk neckerchief made from the cocoon by their own hands. Whoever reads this Journal will be bound to own that the Brethren were blest with as good and industrious and kind sisters as can be found.

The men's neckerchiefs were collar-width, with a small bow in the front and with the fastening in the back. And the regular white silk handkerchiefs for men were made for the market and priced at a dollar each.

The women's kerchiefs, 32 by 34 inches, were worn around the shoulders, folded in a triangle. Some were solid colors—white, blue, mulberry, or light or dark brown. Others were checked, and still others had a twilled border or a border of contrasting color. Kerchiefs of changeable color were made of the floss, thus "saving all the cocoon."

So successful were the South Union sisters that for several years in the 1840s the Shaker community of North Union, Ohio, sent their cocoons to be reeled at South Union "where they are skilled in the art." Finally in June 1848 two of the South Union sisters went to North Union to teach the art of reeling and spinning silk.

The Kentucky Shakers sold silk to the eastern societies, even though its cost "might seem middling high." Often the silk kerchiefs were presented as gifts to eastern visitors or were taken as gifts by the Kentucky leaders when they went east on official visits. Once a South Union gift for each of the sisters consisted of needles full of silk, the thread being wound on a small piece of paper and put into a little fruit bowl to be handed around.

Not only did the Kentucky leaders send samples of their silk to other Shakers, but pride in their silk prompted the elders to send samples to the editors of national publications.

The *Niles Register* for March 26, 1831, reported:

Since our last publication in which we made a few remarks on the cultivation of silk, we have been politely furnished with beautiful specimens of white and blue sewing silk, and very strong but plain ribbands, made at the Shakers' establishment near Harrodsburg in Kentucky. The sewing silks are as smooth and even as any we ever examined and very soft and fine.

These neat and industrious and harmless people, however, cultivate and manufacture silk only for their own use.

And in 1833 when Elder Benjamin wrote to renew South Union's subscription to the *American Farmer*, he enclosed four skeins of silk with the instructions that two were for the editor J. J. Hitchcock, and one each for Gideon B. Smith and J. S. Skinner.

Although the silk industry was left chiefly to the sisters, the brethren did help by keeping the looms in working order and by setting up new looms. It was worthy of a journal entry when Samuel McClelland got his new silk loom into operation and "it worked handsomely."

Society visitors found the silk culture fascinating. A Virginian visiting at Pleasant Hill in 1825 found that "sewing silk of superior quality was raised there." In *American Vinedressers' Guide* (Cincinnati, Ohio, 1826) John J. Dufour wrote that the silk of the Mercer County Shakers was "preferred by the taylors to any imported."

A Rebel cavalryman whose group stopped at South Union in February 1862 said to Eldress Nancy, "You wear silk, and do you not buy that?" "Nay," she replied, "we make all our own silk. We raise the worms, spin and weave the silk." The soldier thought it was "very nice anyhow."

Another distinctive industry carried on by the women was that of making their summer bonnets and the brethren's hats from field straw. Any hollow straw, such as rye and oats, that could be flattened and split into narrow strips could be used.

When the straw reached the right stage, several women would go to the field, carefully cut the straws, and bring them back to the laundry in large flat baskets. After two rounds of scalding the straws in large kettles of boiling water followed by hours of bleaching in the sun, the straws were given a sulfur bleach. This was achieved by spreading the straws over a slotted tray and placing it in a box containing a pot of hot coals to which sulfur had been added.

After remaining covered twenty-four hours, the straws were removed and thoroughly rinsed. While damp they were placed on some flat surface so each could be split open with a pin. Next the sisters pulled each flattened straw through a little wire-toothed straw splitter, thus obtaining the narrow strands for weaving.

After the bonnet front and crown were cut from the woven yardage, a small wire was run around the edge of the front. Then the two parts or "chips" were sewn together and the whole was dampened and placed on the wooden bonnet block to be dried into shape. The last steps were to cover the wire and the seam with a straw braid or a narrow piece of cloth and to attach pleated flounces or tails and bonnet ties of silk or cotton.

The men's hats were made by fastening together braided lengths of straw and shaping the crown on a wooden hat block. Measurements were approximately five inches deep for the crown and four to four and one-half inches for the brim.

Journal entries give evidence that the hats and bonnets were made not only for home use but for the market as well. "Mch. 23, 1835. <u>Trading Trip.</u> U. E. Johns set off this morning for the city of Nashville with 300 hats made by the sisters."

By the spring of 1839 palm leaf was being used as well as straw, the Kentucky sisters having learned the art of palm leaf weaving from "their gospel friends in New Lebanon, N.Y." They also learned that straw bonnets could be strengthened by weaving the straw into a palm warp. Palm leaf fans were made and added to the sales items.

The women's work was appreciated and given considerable space in the daily records. It was recounted how the South Union sisters "took up the flax off the meadow after it was well rotted and ready for the break," and the writer added, "It is just and proper to note that the young sisters turn out in the flax-pulling to do a faithful part in it."

It was also recorded that Eldress Betsy being "very unwell with a severe pain in her stomach and bowels, still stirred around saying that she had no time to be sick." How much more dedicated could a sister or brother be? In 1835 Elder Benjamin wrote in his journal that "the sisters had done a faithful and good part toward paying off the public land debt." A later elder, Harvey L. Eads, agreed: "I can say for them that they are as faithful, industrious, kind and generous and in every way as worthy as the brethren."

One of the first and most profitable industries of all the American Shakers was marketing packaged garden seeds. It was an industry that required much time and effort from both men and women. Following the practice of the older societies, the Kentucky Shakers set aside entire fields for the raising of vegetable seeds. Often there were several varieties of one vegetable, the principal one being cabbage. In 1858 one could choose from Large Drumhead, Early York, Large Early, Flat Dutch, and Green Curled Savoy cabbage. On the 1866 South Union order sheets, varieties of peas included Extra Early, Early May, Tom Thumb, White Marrowfat, and Daniel O'Rourke.

Some varieties of seeds remained constant on the annual lists, while others were dropped in favor of new ones. As one trustee put it, "We do not aim to have an extensive variety of seeds, but cultivate those which we know to be valuable." It was also emphasized that the packaged seeds were mostly grown in the societies. When demand made it necessary, however, the trustees would purchase additional seed from reliable sources. It was made clear that all seeds were tested and "none would be sent out but what germinate." Some of the seeds planted in society fields were imported from England and Scotland. One shipment of Early York cabbage seed from Dods in Scotland reached South Union in June 1835, and some were planted immediately. A short time later it was reported that the seeds had "come up well sprouted, strong, and looked thrifty." Thus the Scottish seeds passed the germination test.

Raising great quantities of seed for the market was not a simple process. The seeds had to be harvested and cleaned. Thousands of packets had to be cut from large rolls of paper and printed one at a time on a small handpress. Explicit planting instructions were printed on each seed packet. For example, J. R. Bryant of Pleasant Hill gave instructions for planting the white lima or butter bean: "The Lima Bean requires a richer soil than other varieties—are very tender and should not be planted in the open ground before the 1st or 2nd week

33

in May, and not more than about half inch deep as they incline to rot in cool or moist situations. The poles should be 3 or 4 feet apart."

The women attended to the folding of the small papers, which then had to be filled and sealed, ready to be arranged in wooden boxes the men had made. "Oct. 11, 1832. A big evening job—8 brethren after supper made complete 100 boxes before midnight." Only a few days before, the society had boxed a total of 50,275 packets in 224 boxes.

The seeds were sold at seven cents per package until Civil War times, when the price had to be lowered to five cents. By the 1840s Pleasant Hill was selling bluegrass seed, and in 1896 South Union shipped twenty bushels of peach seeds to the McGinnis nursery in Bowling Green.

The earliest seed trading trips were made chiefly in the home districts. A Shaker merchant would fill his saddlebags with seed papers and ride out for several days. On the longer wagon trips two brothers, or one brother with a youth for company, usually went driving a two-horse team. If the roads were known to be very bad, the seed trip might be made with a six-horse team. Such was the case in 1827 when South Union sent a load of seeds to Harmony and Busroe, Indiana. Eventually, regular routes were established in Tennessee, Georgia, Alabama, and Louisiana.

Early in 1816 Francis Voris and Absalom Fite of Pleasant Hill started down to New Orleans—according to the journal, "the first of the brethren that went to New Orleans." It was not recorded how they went nor what they took to sell, but it is highly probable that their main purpose was to explore the possibilities of river trading, for in the 1820s both Kentucky societies began a program of flatboat trips along the southern waterways.

At first the South Union brothers loaded their produce in wagons and drove either thirty miles to Red River or sixty miles to the Cumberland at Clarksville, Tennessee. There they transferred their produce to a flatboat, which they had either built themselves or had hired built. After the Kentucky legislature voted to build locks on the Barren and Green rivers, the South Union trips could begin closer home on the Barren at Bowling Green or on the Green at Bellars Landing.

The Pleasant Hill merchants loaded their boats at their own Kentucky River landing and then plied their way downriver to Port William, later called Carrollton, where they entered the Ohio. Often the Pleasant Hill merchants went to Saint Louis or turned off into the Arkansas River and went "away to the wilds of the West, expecting to find a market among the Indians." South Union usually went directly to New Orleans.

The Shaker traders from both societies maintained contacts in all the river towns. Sometimes they would tie up long enough for one of the crew to walk to an inland town where he called on the merchants.

Sometimes merchants from the two villages crossed paths. In 1836 Brother Urban wrote back to South Union from Vicksburg: "There is six of the Pleasant Hill brethren in this country at this time. We can hear of them going up every river and bayou . . . thus you see they leave no hole for us. We would not wish you to think that we are discouraged and sunk in our feelings, there is nothing of it. We expect to do the best we know how and return home."

The unexpected competition seems to have obscured Urban's view somewhat. The truth was that the smaller sales they were experiencing were related more to the emerging financial panic of 1837 than to the sales made by the other Kentuckians. The following year it was noted in the Pleasant Hill journal that although "vast quantities of our produce has been shipped down the Ohio and Mississippi rivers to the New Orleans market, the price of our produce is very little over one half what it was a year ago."

Later it was stated that "the merchants do not give a very flattering account of the 'one thing needful' "—that is, money. The 1840s and 1850s brought a return of better sales, but they dipped again during the Civil War period.

The river trips were arranged to start in late October or early November, and the merchants would be gone from two to four months. Although the trips were scheduled primarily for selling seeds, the merchants left home with numerous other salable items, such as coopers' wares, brooms, carpeting, jeans, tow linen, linsey, straw hats and bonnets, stockings and "footens," and candlewicks.

The Pleasant Hill journals contain more references to sweetmeats, confectionery, and herbs than do those of South Union; whereas flour, potatoes, and onions seem to have been special sales items for South Union.

Both societies sent along some livestock on the early seed trips, but after the coming of the steamboats, Pleasant Hill made many trips for the sole purpose of taking cattle to Saint Louis, New Orleans, and other river markets. The cattle would be driven to Louisville for loading. At least once the trip came to a sudden end when "they sold out in Louisville."

Trips to the Nashville markets were made overland. The Pleasant Hill men sometimes stopped by South Union to rest and to be joined for a double drive on to Nashville.

The successful sales attest to the high regard accorded the celibate Shakers for their ability in breeding livestock. By 1822 the South Union trustees had purchased Comet, their first fine Durham bull. A few weeks later Comet was found dead—"by drinking water from the little house." Later the trustees went to the "upper Kentucky counties" and purchased Orion for one thousand dollars. Now and then the society trustees exchanged animals. For example, "Hooper took Orion to the bank of Green river, met Brother Stephen of Pleasant Hill and exchanged the bull for 'Dunn Duff,' Pleasant Hill's bull."

As early as 1811 the Pleasant Hill society had joint ownership with Union Village of the bull named Shaker. They also used Buzzard. Both of these animals were prominent in the herd books of that time.

The Pleasant Hill men were familiar figures around the early stock fairs in Lexington and Winchester, and they seldom missed the Woodford County sales of "Alexander's blooded cattle." On September 2, 1856, they purchased two head of the stock, one being for South Union.

In April 1859, when William Runyon and C. Todd went to Alexander's to get Sirius, it was presumably not to purchase but to make arrangements for stud service.

A letter written from Pleasant Hill to New Lebanon on June 14, 1834, contained the information that

our cattle are considered by stock raisers to be very good. In 1833 we sold stock to the amount of $1,942. Last year not quite so much. Our full-blood Durhams are in great demand but we cannot spare any of them yet.

We sell our mixed-blood cows and heifers from $25–100 per head. Bull cows from $50–100 per head. Oxen $50–75 per pair.

Not only their Durham cattle, but also their Merino, Cotswold, and Bakewell sheep and their Berkshire hogs were greatly desired by farmers both in Kentucky and in neighboring states.

Sometimes stock was bartered. For example, in 1821 South Union purchased a new carding machine "with 3 horses valued at $400." In 1857 Pleasant Hill took some cattle to the Swedish colony of Bishop Hill in Illinois. Since the men brought back a new carriage made at Bishop Hill, it seems likely that there was some exchanging done. Another entry of the same period indicates that it was a time of financial stress, for Micajah Burnett "sold mostly on credit" in the Illinois territory, there being "the greatest pressure on the money market that has been experienced since the Revolutionary War."

The men and boys who left their respective societies to market various products never knew what experiences they might have during the weeks and months they would be traveling. There is evidence that both the traders and the home society felt a need to keep in touch. Before leaving on a long trip, the merchants were given dates and places where they could expect a letter, and in turn they promised to mail letters home from specified stops.

When Jefferson Shannon arrived in Vicksburg in late December 1830, he was happy to find a letter from South Union. It was good to learn that the society had acquired five more horses, that the East family brick shop had been finished, and that Elder Benjamin had gone to Frankfort to join the Pleasant Hill leaders in their effort to have two Kentucky statutes concerning the Shakers repealed or amended. It was also comforting to know that the sisters sent their love and good wishes to the brothers "so far off in a wild and friendless country."

A letter sent from South Union on December 13, 1838, brought heart-warming news that the home society would "dance a song for you in our Christmas meeting—all wish you to think of home at that time and see if you can feel our spirits." No doubt "union" was achieved on that special day.

Letters sent home by the merchants brought news of the traders' health, the economic condition of the territory, a description of unusual places and events, information concerning all crops and mechanical devices that were new to them, and now and then an admission of homesickness. However, one who wrote of his anxiety to get home added "as we have set out to sell or dispose of garden seed, we feel that it would be best to accomplish that duty first in the best manner we are able."

The Shaker merchants seemed to have been blessed with unusually good health. Although there were reported cases of colds, severe insect stings, sore eyelids, and extreme weariness from wagon travel over poor roads or from long confinement on a flatboat, there were only two recorded cases of serious illness on the sales trips. In 1834, during the first serious cholera epidemic, Jesse McComb of South Union died of cholera in Saint Louis. And in January 1856, E. W. Scott of Pleasant Hill was detained in New Orleans "being confined two or three weeks with the yellow fever."

During the second epidemic of cholera early in 1849, business operations were mostly suspended in New Orleans; so Micajah Burnett had "to store away his confectionery and leave it unsold." Fourteen deaths occurred from cholera on board the boat on which he arrived home in good health. A follow-up trip had to be made in March to dispose of the Pleasant Hill "confectionery."

The South Union brethren also traveled on a boat where several died of cholera, but "so confident and unconcerned for themselves they were that the world themselves did not believe the Shakers would take it or be attacked by it."

The traders were often affected by the extremes of nature. Low water on the Arkansas River once detained two Pleasant Hill brothers, and high water, which destroyed a bridge, forced two South Union men to turn back from a wagon trip to Nashville.

It was in February 1855 that J. R. Bryant returned from Louisville, reporting that Micajah Burnett was icebound at the mouth of the Kentucky River with his cargo and cattle on hand, "the Ohio river being completely frozen over." A month earlier E. W. Scott had been blocked by ice near Smithland, Kentucky. So he "made a pedestrian tramp of about forty miles where he intercepted a stage" which took him to South Union. There he was delayed several days before continuing his journey to Mercer County.

Disaster could come in the form of a sinking boat. Such was the news received in a letter written by Elhanon on December 1, 1845, to the Pleasant Hill ministry, saying that the boat they were on got snagged and sank in about fifteen minutes. Fortunately they were near shore and no lives were lost. They managed to save their clothes and cattle "except one little calf."

Later, news was received that "Elhanon by hard labor got his preserves and sweetmeats out of the sunken boat but part of them were stolen before he could get them on board another boat."

During the same season, misfortune befell two South Union merchants—Eli McLean and George Waddle. The boat on which Eli was traveling exploded and he was thrown upon the boiler and badly burned. Later "some wretch robbed him of six dollars." Meanwhile the boat on which George had passage sank, but he sustained no loss except being detained.

It was in January 1865 that the *Eleanor Carrol* burned at the Louisville wharf. On board was a Pleasant Hill shipment of preserves and seeds valued at $1,100. Fortunately the goods were insured at full value, and the society was "paid without the trouble of taking them to Orleans." The journalist could have added there was a saving in expenses and time as well as in trouble.

Not only the river merchants but those who traveled the roadways could meet with reverses. It might be the "villainous mayor" of Lexington, who in 1838 demanded ten dollars for "retailing seed within the corporation," or the many guerrillas who beset the Shaker brothers in 1864 and 1865 when they resumed their trading journeys. "Mch. 15, 1865. Return. Elder Wm. Ware returned. Not having the precaution to send his money all by express, when about fifty miles from home, he was robbed of the sum of $150.00 and his best horse—but returned safe in person. He had previously sent by Express—$500.00." During this period there was always rejoicing when the merchants having run the gauntlet of guerrilla warfare returned in safety.

The Shaker merchants always brought home a great variety of essential items which were either not produced at all by the societies or produced in insufficient quantity. Among the purchases were sugar, tea, coffee, sweet oil, fulling mill dyes (e.g., logwood, fustick, madder, and red tarter), spun cotton, trimming for the "great coats," darning needles and thimbles, tin pans and funnels, tableware, glass tumblers, butter plates, brass clocks, and chamber pots. Listed also were leather, steel, sheet iron, screws, nails, awl blades, handsaw files, and barlow knives.

Among the items bought for use in the society schools were slate pencils, steel pens, pencils, tin cups, and New Testaments and Bibles.

One trading trip to Danville in 1816 by a Pleasant Hill trustee yielded two yards of velvet, one looking glass, one padlock, two gimlets, three files, one stick bottle-green twist, and some bed cord. In 1820 a South Union merchant returned home with bowls, cups and saucers, pitchers, teapots, and coffee pots. No doubt the growing membership created the need for purchasing additional household items, for many of the newcomers had little to add to the community supplies.

When such items as tableware and the other things listed above appear in today's Shaker exhibits, it should be understood that they were "Shaker used" rather than "Shaker made."

The Shaker brothers who went out in wagons returned with their wagons loaded with their purchases. But those who went down the river in flatboats sold the boats in the port city and returned with their supplies aboard a steamboat. Landing in either Nashville or Louisville the traders were met by wagons from their respective villages.

Upon their arrival back in the home society the merchants reported on their trip directly to the ministry. Later the society would honor the men with a gathering and sing welcome songs composed for the occasion. Such songs underscored the society belief that God watched over those who put their hands to the work of marketing and "blest them on their way."

With the coming of the railroad and the beginning of widespread commercial manufacturing, changes in Shaker trading practices were inevitable. Faster and cheaper means of trading had to be found if Shaker goods were to compete with those being machine produced.

The new railroad was seen as making it possible to send out a single trustee to solicit orders which could be shipped later by rail or by a combination of train and boat. The solicitor himself might travel by stage, boat, train, or any combination of these.

The South Union Shakers were particularly favored with rail service, since the Memphis branch of the Louisville and Nashville railroad had been completed across their land in 1860. The trustees themselves had established a railway center less than a mile from the heart of the village. There they built a depot which they rented to the railroad company. Also they built and rented out a store building. Although they moved their post office from the village proper to the railway center, one of the brothers remained the appointed postmaster until 1888 when "politics carried the day," and a man of the neighborhood was appointed.

Shipment by railroad proved especially profitable for getting flour and vegetables to market while still fresh. It was an easier way to transport the heavy wooden boxes of preserves, which had been rather cumbersome for the wagons, and shipments increased. The South Union trustees also found it convenient to order their glass preserve jars shipped by the carload from Saint Louis or Cincinnati. The jars came stamped with the words *Shaker Preserves*. Sometimes *South Union* was also stamped on the glass.

Believing that doing well economically was worshiping God aright, the Shaker trustees were interested in all mechanical devices that might help expedite the work and free some of the brothers and sisters for other tasks. In the early days, the American Shakers had invented many needed devices, such as the press for making flat brooms and a double stove to increase heating capacity. They had also taken some of the world's inventions and improved on them—the early washing machine, for example. The Kentucky Shakers added their own inventions—at Pleasant Hill a one-tongued wagon; at South Union an apple corer and a window sash balance to improve ventilation.

But when the machine age arrived, the Shaker trustees examined the new factory-produced farm implements and bought those they believed would be of benefit, such as the seven-point plow, grain reapers, or seed separators.

Sometimes the society simply rented a machine. For example, in July 1884 the South Union trustees "hired a thresher which threshed 5,000 bushels at four cents per bushel."

So for over a century Mother Ann's western children sought to create a utopian society. Being a pragmatic people, not merely idle dreamers, they came to be known for their accomplishments in agriculture and architecture, in manufacturing and trading. Accepting their work program as an integral part of their religion, the Kentucky Shakers put their hands to work while giving their hearts to God.

3

GIVING THEIR
HEARTS TO GOD

THE RELIGIOUS TENETS of the American Shakers were based
both on the teachings of Mother Ann Lee and on the New
Testament teachings of Christ.

Samuel Hurlburt of South Union once phrased the Shaker
beliefs in the style of an advertisement:

SHAKERS WANTED

100,000 Shakers wanted. . . . none need apply who cannot learn to
shake themselves free from all prejudices, all wrong, all sin, all evil of
every name and nature.

But all who apply bringing with them the following credentials will
be welcomed as inquirers and given every facility to learn.

The credentials or characteristics listed were a willing-
ness to confess all sins and to live a pure virgin life, a desire to
find a refuge from social evil by living a communal life, and an
understanding that the Shaker way was one of industry, honesty, simplicity.

The Shaker beliefs were written into the society covenants
and into the published works and were expounded by the
ministry in regular meetings. But the ordinary member was
governed less by the formal pronouncements of the later leaders than by the oral teachings of Mother Ann and the other

early leaders. These familiar admonitions, worn smooth by constant repetition, became the daily guidelines to true Shakerism.

Industry
   Do all your work as if you had a thousand years to live and as if you were to die tomorrow.

Honesty
   Be what we seem to be; and seem to be what we really are; don't carry two faces.

Thrift and Charity
   Be prudent and saving . . . so you may have wherewith to give to them that stand in need.

Cleanliness
   Clean your room well, for good spirits will not live where there is dirt.

Order
   A place for everything and everything in its place.

Health
   Let none abstain from food which they need; eat hearty and do the will of God.

Functionalism
   That which has in itself the highest use possesses the greatest beauty.

The constant daily application of the practical tenets, coupled with the acceptance of such doctrines as the male/female duality of God, the confession of sin, pacifism, and the community of goods, placed strenuous demands on the new converts. As a result the leaders discouraged a too-hasty surrender to Shakerism. No one could sign the covenant and become a member of the church or senior family before he was twenty-one. It was also written into the covenant that "none are permitted to sign it until they have counted well the cost; or at least pondered for a time upon its requirements."

It was often pointed out that not everybody was "prepared or able to live so angelic a life" and that "an idle, lazy person will not long abide in the society."

Newcomers were generally placed in the gathering or junior order, usually called the East family. There they were instructed for a year by senior members, while entering into the society work program and participating in the church worship services. During this probationary period their property was inventoried and managed by the society.

There were those, however, who insisted on living in their own natural family group and managing their own temporal affairs. Such was the case at South Union in May 1821, when a double log cabin was raised where Robert Pearce and his family were to live until Leah, the wife, might consent to join.

As late as August 18, 1880, a trustee had "to fix up the tan house" for Francis Montfort, a miller, who came from Tunnel Hill with his wife and three children. It was reported that Francis wanted to live a Shaker life but his wife was not ready. After living in the "halfway house" for a month, the Montforts were admitted into the society.

Those who decided to become covenant members gave over their property to the trustees. Some had little to contribute, while others brought household goods, wagons, teams, cows, and possibly pigs and chickens. Many had land. If the land was close enough, it was incorporated into the society lands, but if it was at a distance, it was sold and the proceeds placed in the communal treasury.

Some brought their slaves, posing an ethical problem for the ministry, who found slave-holding contrary to their humanistic teachings. By 1815 or 1816 the elders in both Kentucky societies began an intensive program on the necessity of freeing the slaves and releasing the children. Each man who was persuaded to free his slaves was counseled to write a statement on parchment and to sign it. Then he was to have it countersigned by the civil court and recorded in the clerk's office. For example, in a statement drawn up in 1832 for forty-three-year-old Hannah Dickerow, Hannah was "hereby . . . manumitted, tolerated, and set free and forever hereafter to enjoy her freedom as though she had been born free, and is moreover discharged from the performance of any contract entered into during her servitude."

Some who freed their slaves did so with limitations. Thomas McLean was willing to free his blacks only if they agreed to leave Kentucky and "fix their residence in Ohio, Illinois or Indiana."

When the slaves were given over to the society, liberation papers were drawn up immediately. But money that had been earned by "slave hire and sale" was never accepted. When Daniel and Thornton Whyte entered the South Union society in 1830, they gave over their Hopkins County lands to the trustees, but they assigned their cash holdings made through slavery to "some emancipating society or other like charitable uses and purposes."

Not all slave-holding novitiates could be persuaded to subscribe to abolition. In July 1816, while attending a South Union meeting related to the freeing of slaves, James Judkins said he would go back to the world rather than see his slaves freed. It is little wonder that his slaves wished to remain in the society. Judkins agreed to sell Sampson, Old Molly, Lucy, and Violett to the society for $800 to be paid in four annual installments. The journal entry for September 25 read, "When Judkins left for his old nest, he looked up every old horseshoe that once was his—good he will need them all."

The Pleasant Hill trustees also purchased slaves as an act of charity. One such slave was Anthony Chism who had become a Believer in 1806. For forty-one years he had walked three miles to Pleasant Hill to attend Sunday and holy day services. When he was purchased, he was placed in the West family as a full member.

There was also Jonas Crutcher, a Believer for nineteen years, who was hired at Pleasant Hill with his wages being paid to his owner. Hearing that the owner was moving out of the area, the trustees asked to purchase Jonas so he would have the privilege of being "one of the brethren on equal terms with the rest of us." When Jonas died three years later, it was written that "he was much respected and beloved in the family where he resided, which love was not misplaced for he was worthy."

46

Elder Harvey Lauderdale Eades. Brought to South Union as a baby in 1807, Eades became one of the most prominent members of the community. He died in 1892.
Courtesy of Kentucky Library, Western Kentucky University

Jane Cowan, the last woman trustee at South Union. In addition to running the poultry business, she kept records and corresponded with the other Shaker societies.

Eldress Virginia Breedlove. Brought to South Union by her widowed mother Harriet, who also became an eldress. Eldress Virginia died in 1909.

Courtesy of the Western Reserve Historical Society Library

Willow basket used for collecting herbs. This willow work was done only at Pleasant Hill.

Courtesy of Shakertown at Pleasant Hill

Large blue oval box. Ordinarily Shakers did not mark personal possessions, but in later days names sometimes appeared.   *Private collection*

Kentucky Shaker straw bonnet
Courtesy of National Gallery of Art
Index of American Design

Straw splitter, used in the manufacture of bonnets, hats, and needlebook covers
Courtesy of South Union
Shaker Museum

BEAN,

WHITE LIMA, or BUTTER.

The Lima Bean requires a richer soil than other varieties—are very tender, and should not be planted, in the open ground, before the 1st or 2nd week in May, and not more than about half inch deep, as they incline to rot in cool or moist situations. The poles should be 3 or 4 feet apart.

J. R. Bryant Pleasant Hill, Ky.

WINTER TURNEP,

Makes the best and earliest greens in the Spring of any vegetable. Sow at the end of Summer or early in the Fall, in light rich soil, and in drills 18 in. apart. Hoe when the leaves are two or three inches long, and when the plants are somewhat larger hoe again, & thin them to 9 in. apart. When sown broadcast in the field they are excellent for sheep.

South Union, Ky.

Seed packets and seed box
Courtesy of Susan Jackson Keig, James Ballard, and E. Ray Pearson

with both fancier and farmer." Their plumage is white, heavily laced with black; the lacing on the breast is peculiarly handsome. They have a small rose comb, close fitting; face and ear lobes bright red. Hens weigh six and a half pounds, when full grown. If allowed to sit they make most careful mothers, are content anywhere and will not fly ower a fence four feet high. Of course they will not breed as true as some of the older varieties. A few of the chicks, too, have single combs, (which is true of all rose comb varieties), but as we weed these out, we expect less each season. Will have no birds for sale before spring.

Brown Leghorns.

We often hear the question asked: "Which do you think is the best breed of fowls?" If eggs are desired, without regard to the quality, or quantity, or style of poultry for the table, we expect an answer might be given in favor of the Leghorn. It is said by the admirers of this breed that they will lay eggs until their bodies seem actually to fall away, and their combs and wattels shrivel as though the blood had been exhausted. Now we don't pretend to vouch for the truth of this assertion, as this is the first season we have bred them, and as yet have had no opportunity to test their merits. But when a small or medium sized fowl commences in the latter part of winter or early spring with the tendency and instinct, or natural habit, to lay one egg a day, and follow it up for months with only short intervals, and without sitting, there is a very great draft on the vital forces. The nutriment contained in the egg must

Page from Harvey Eades' *Farm Annual*, probably 1885
Courtesy of Old Chatham Shaker Library

Group of Shakers at west side of Pleasant Hill's Centre House,
about 1890   *Courtesy of Susan Jackson Keig*

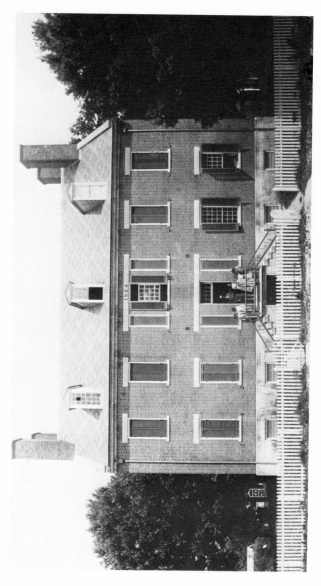

Centre House at South Union, before 1922. Fancy roof was a late Shaker replacement for earlier black-oak shingle and tin roofs.

Courtesy of Western Reserve Historical Society

At Pleasant Hill the blacks lived in the various family houses, but since South Union was more surrounded by slave owners, it was found advisable there to establish a separate black family, who occupied a number of cabins at the west side of the village. A special dining room for the blacks was built onto the south end of the frame office building.

Some apprehension was felt that once the parchments had been made out and given to the slaves, there would be a full exit. This did not prove to be the case, for few had either the means or the experience to survive as free blacks in Kentucky or even to support themselves in any of the free states.

One who did leave South Union was Sampson Anderson. Returning from a seed trip to New Orleans, Sampson quit his companions in Nashville to take a steamboat job. When he was admonished about deserting the cause, he exclaimed, "Talk to me about Eternal Hope! Why Jesus Christ never saw a steam boat."

The journals at both South Union and Pleasant Hill reveal the continuing concern felt over slavery by the ministries. Although the Shaker societies were not participants in the Kentucky Colonization Society's work, they were alert to its activities.

We read in a Pleasant Hill entry dated May 10, 1857: "A company of Negroes, thirty-five in number which William Thompson one of our near and best neighbors had manumitted for the purpose of sending them to Liberia, passed through this place enroute for that happy land of freedom, which they could not find in the renowned state of Kentucky which boasts so highly of liberty and human rights."

Hiring slave labor was always distasteful to the Shaker leaders, but in their large expansion program they found their need for extra help so critical that the practice had been tolerated.

When emancipation became a reality throughout the nation, the Kentucky Shakers were able to pay wages directly to their hired laborers, not to the masters. It was recorded with relief that "the colored man Jordan who drove our ox team last year and for which service we paid his master is now driving the same team for which we are to pay him at the end of the year's service."

Some covenant members found it difficult to accord their former slaves their full human rights. To help change this attitude and to foster spiritual growth in general, each ministry conducted a regular schedule of worship services. Weekday mornings before breakfast each family held a meditation service in the meeting room of its own dwelling. Also singing meetings were often arranged one evening a week in the separate families.

On Sundays the entire village met in the meetinghouse for two worship services, one in the morning at nine, the other at "candle-lighting time." In keeping with their dual precept, "Put your hands to work and give your hearts to God," the worship services were often a combination of business reports by the trustees, the reading of letters from other societies, and sermons by the ministry.

Included also was the singing or laboring of hymns. On occasion portions from theological works like *The Testimony of Christ's Second Coming* or the *Precepts of Mother Ann Lee* were read aloud. New Testament teachings were also stressed.

During the summer or fall months there was an eleven o'clock Sunday service opened to "the world." Usually there were more visitors than could be accommodated inside the meetinghouse. If, as often happened, the public were inattentive or showed amusement, the announced meetings would be canceled for the rest of the season.

At the public meetings the sermons were designed less for the members than for the visitors who sat impatiently waiting the time when the portable, backless seats would be stacked and the society dancing would begin.

Many travelers to Kentucky made a point of visiting one or the other of the two Shaker villages, hoping always to attend a service. The journal kept by Andrew Broaddus of Virginia on his trip to Kentucky in the fall of 1817 contains his eye-witness account of a South Union service.

The meeting was held in the first meetinghouse, which consisted of two rooms that opened into one by means of a sliding partition.

The men formed in rows, making a solid column in one room; the women facing them in the same manner in the other; and the communication was opened. They stood in silence two or three minutes, and then broke forth in a loud and melodious manner; in singing an anthem, which might last ten minutes. Then changing their position, they stood in readiness for the sacred dance; the men in rows facing their row of singers, and the women in a similar attitude. The musick began with a lively, animating and pleasing tone, and the dance went on in complete unison with the time. Words composed for the occasion, in lively rhyme, soon followed. The . . . singers grew more animated, keeping time by stamping with the foot; while the dancers went on with answerable animation, traversing the room up and down, backwards and forwards, and sometimes facing about, with a simultaneous motion. At certain quick parts of the time the singers strike the time by several loud clappings.

Presently a pause was made, and all stood still for nearly a minute. A new tune was struck up, verse soon followed; and the same kind of exercise went on.

After the meeting closed, one of the Shaker brothers said to Broaddus, "Well, you have now seen the worst of it, there is nothing in our meetings worse than you have seen."

Broaddus, who was a Baptist minister, recorded in his diary that there was "an appearance of solemnity and devotion as well as animation, which one would hardly expect to find, judging from common report."

In the early days, before each village could construct its trustees' office, accommodating a number of overnight visitors could be burdensome. The South Union entry for February 3, 1812, carries a note of annoyance. "Strangers. We have, almost daily, strangers to entertain. In the two nights past we have had 28 strangers. This morning 12 horses were saddled before the door."

The visitors were not always strangers. In May 1811, the well-known Methodist circuit rider Peter Cartwright came with two of his colleagues—John Lewis and John Travis. Certainly Barton Stone, their former archenemy, was not a stranger when he arrived at South Union for a visit in March 1825.

That same year Pleasant Hill had a Virginia visitor who attended a Sunday service and later set down his experience. Arriving in the village about eleven o'clock, he heard a "doleful noise." Learning that the Shakers were at worship, he tied his horse and hastened into the meetinghouse, where he found about 130 worshipers, including men and women, black and white.

He noted the uniform dress of the women, "long-waisted gowns of dark color, long checked aprons extending to the neck, a white long-eared cap, with a white kerchief thrown over the shoulders, crossed and pinned before and a checked cotton handkerchief loosely hung over the arm."

The men were dressed in suits of light-colored domestic cloth, "with coats and waistcoats of the long-waisted fashion, with outer pockets in the former, half-way down the legs, and those in the waistcoats resting on the hips. Their shirts were of coarse cotton." The Virginian probably found it surprising to see blacks of each sex "arranged indiscriminately in the same ranks and attired in the same manner with the whites."

Later in his "Letters from Kentucky," this visitor (name unknown) gave a detailed account of the marching and laboring and the effect on himself.

Two singers from each sex now took their stands at the head of their correspondent columns. A signal being given, the singers commenced and the columns got into motion.

They gently advanced and receded for some minutes, when on a sudden they reversed fronts, quickened their manner and danced in a similar manner. Suddenly they whirled to their former positions increasing in the violence of their actions, as they were warmed by the spirit and animated by the singing. By one impulse they now broke order in which they stood and each column whirled within its own limits, in vertical commotion, throwing their heads, hands, and legs in wild disorder, occasionally leaping up and uttering a horrid yell. . . .

Shrieks and yells followed in alternate succession till by their violence and incessant fury of their dancing, the worshippers were exhausted. Some sank to the floor, whilst others were scarce able to get to their seats.

The meeting closed and the visitor left the house "with feelings of horror" which, he said, the reader could better imagine than he could describe. The singing was "*Vox Nil Praeterea*, sound without words, rhyme, or sense."

Although the Pleasant Hill Shakers were using a wordless march at this particular 1825 service, it was more customary for the Kentucky Shakers to labor or march one of the many new western hymns. From the earliest days in Ohio and Kentucky, the leaders, especially Richard McNemar, had composed texts. And the members who had been singers of revival hymns were quick to adopt the new ones with their strong rhythm and simple texts.

Typical stanzas were

> *I want to feel little*
> *I want to be low,*
> *I want Mother's blessings*
> *Wherever I go.*

or

> *I'll be simple, I'll be lowly,*
> *   In it flows such heav'nly mirth,*
> *To be humble, to be holy*
> *   Is the prettiest thing on earth.*

Many of the texts were copied into the society journals. On June 11, 1815, Elder Benjamin wrote down what he called the "well-known Revival song."

> *Come old and young, come great and small.*
> *There's love and union free for all,*
> *And everyone that will obey*
> *Has now a right to dance and play.*

> *For dancing is a sweet employ*
> *It fills the soul with heav'nly joy,*
> *It makes our love and union flow*
> *While round and round and round we go.*

The elder noted that "they sung the well-known song, round after round, mid shaking, rejoicing, stamping and turning."

Many hymns were exchanged through correspondence. In a letter sent from Pleasant Hill to South Union on December 30, 1834, mention is made of "the beautiful Christmas Hymn" which Eldress Molly Goodrich had sent to Eldress Anna Cole. The writer said, "It is thought to be a charming good hymn." Later a Pleasant Hill writer spoke of a hymn received from New Lebanon, saying, "It is now one of our principal songs in worship." In exchange the writer sent back a new march called "Mother's March" because it had been given a few days before Beloved Mother Ann's birthday. The march, given to Phillip Houser, "came to him spontaneously."

By 1813 the first Shaker hymnal, *Millennial Praises*, had been published in the Hancock, Massachusetts society. It contained both eastern and western songs. In 1833 Richard McNemar of Ohio published *A Selection of Hymns and Poems*. Many of the hymns included were mnemonic, such as the one called "The Covenant." Another written to benefit the gathering order was a song called "A Declaration of Junior Membership."

Whereas with the Shakers, at present, I live,
This plain Declaration *I honestly give,*
To show the condition on which we agree—
How I'm to treat them, and how they're to treat me.

To be a good member, my honor's at stake,
That all my old sins I confess and forsake;
And then, as a brother, it is understood
That I be employed in doing some good.

In uniform clothing we're equally dress'd,
And to the same table I go with the rest,
In health and in sickness, as long as I'm here,
In all their enjoyments I equally share.

I am in my senses, I'm candid and free;
There is no imposition practiced on me:

The terms of the gospel I well understand;
I'm bound to observe them, as witness my hand.

Many of the published Shaker hymns had been received by inspiration from the spirit world, having been communicated to an individual either by the supernatural Voice or by the voice of some departed Believer.

The inspiration not only brought about the writing of hymns but it was felt in many other ways. Some individual members received dances; others had dreams or received messages concerning events which had taken place but of which the society had no other knowledge. Later letters or newspapers would bring confirmation.

In the eastern societies many drawings were made under spiritual guidance, but oddly enough no Kentucky Shaker is known to have received an inspirational drawing.

Both Kentucky societies, however, were led by "inspired instrumentality to set aside a small secluded plot of ground" located on the highest point of their land. The plot, generally known as the "Chosen Square," was dedicated as a place where the members could go to identify with the spirit and receive spiritual gifts. At least two formal meetings a year—one in the spring, one in the fall—were to be held at the outdoor sanctuary.

South Union's Holy Ground was a square lot containing about three-fourths of an acre on the top of a rise south of the burying ground. It was fenced and planted in pine and sugar trees.

Pleasant Hill's square, known as Mount Sinai, was south of the meetinghouse. The first meeting was held there on September 26, 1844, a day designated by Governor R. P. Letcher as one of prayer, praise, and thanksgiving throughout the state. Before their second meeting in October the brethren had finished grading Mount Sinai's plain and had sowed it in bluegrass. Only the Believers marched to the outdoor places of worship, where they sat on the ground or stood for as long as three hours.

Among the first Pleasant Hill Shakers to feel extraordinary

spiritual manifestations was the young brother William Runyon. It happened several times during 1819 that William felt compelled, under great power, to go to the meetinghouse and sit down. There he would begin "to beat an alarm . . . beating it with his feet in the most complicated manner." Elder Samuel Turner wrote the New Lebanon ministry describing young Runyon's exercise.

If there had been a drum in the meeting house it would have made no more noise than his feet and hands did. He would beat his hands on the seat where he sat. At the same time his feet would beat, and it roared like thunder . . . then he would be taken upon the floor and would shuffle the marches as compleat as he would beat them with his feet and hands. Could be heard across the road by the first family who shoved up their windows and wondered what it was. We would say in truth it is the most solemn sight we ever did see.

Another young brother was taken "under very compelling power" to go to the shoe cupboards, where he felt an impulse "to take out all the shoes and to brush them very clean and nice." Then he brushed the cupboard, placed the shoes back in order, then took the brush and gathered the dirt all into a heap and was immediately "brought down on his face," from which position he had to lick up the dirt and spit it into the fire before he was released.

One of the late spiritual periods at South Union was in the early 1870s. It was on a February Sabbath in 1872 that "the voice of inspiration declared that Mother Ann with ten thousand angels was present . . . the whole meeting appeared to be filled with a heavenly and divine influence."

A week or so later at dinner Elder Harvey reported that he had seen a beautiful star or light on his hat, brighter than anything he had ever seen. And directly his hat had been covered all over and he had been surrounded with lights. He thought someone present might be able to tell him what it meant. Staying at South Union at that time were several spiritualists from New Orleans, who might have answered. But it was Brother Solomon, not the spiritualists, who said he believed the lights were the good spirits who had come to bless Harvey for his obedience.

With all their daily concern for spiritual matters, the Shakers did not place the same emphasis on special holidays as did their neighbors. The most significant day on the Shaker calendar was Sacrifice Day, which came late in December, or perhaps it was set to coincide with Christmas Day itself. The millennial laws stated that on Sacrifice Day "all Believers should make perfect reconciliation one with another, and leave all grudges, hard feelings, and disaffection toward one another, externally behind on this day." It was also pointed out that "nothing which is this day settled—may hereafter be brought forward against another."

References to Christmas are either missing entirely or very brief. The South Union entry for 1811 reads: "Christmas Believers held meeting. Kept day in songs and dances. Pretty lively." In 1869 the Pleasant Hill society "kept Christmas as the Sabbath. Trained in stepping and shuffling after supper." Evidently the ministry felt that a day without its usual work schedule was a good time to practice their dances.

Although it is not always so recorded, it was customary to hold one general and one union meeting on Christmas and "to remember the poor and to do no work except what was allowed on the Sabbath."

There seems to have been little or no special notice given to Easter. Perhaps the Shaker viewpoint toward this day is reflected somewhat in a 1914 South Union account: "This is Easter Sunday. The outside World are having a great, good time today. Their churches are decorated with Easter lilies and other spring flowers, all this is outside decoration. Hope their souls are to God in some good work and for the suffering and the uplifting of Humanity in some way."

No matter the year or the society, Thanksgiving accounts are all quite similar. After declaring it was a day appointed by the governor, the journalist would outline the day's activities. A typical example is the Pleasant Hill account for 1858. "We arose at half past four. Attended to cleaning up the shop, yards, and premises until half past 9 A.M. Then gathered into the dwelling and kept the day according to Order, had bitten at 11 A.M. Attended general singing meeting at the Center 1 P.M., had supper at 4, after which we went to our temporal employment til 8 P.M. when the bell rang for all to go to rest for the night."

It was not until a late period of Shaker history in Kentucky that the societies began to follow the custom of their neighbors in having a special holiday meal for Thanksgiving Day. In 1876 at South Union the spiritual manifestation was a quiet prayer meeting but "the temporal manifestation was turkey for dinner." By 1894 a South Union elder wrote of "viands on the table . . . both rich and savory."

The Shaker Christmas seasons also came to be marked by change. In an 1891 issue of the Shaker periodical the *Manifesto*, Pleasant Hill reported to "Home Notes": "We had our usual social on Christmas Eve at our school house. A tree laden with fruit made glad the little ones. Had music, songs, and recitations by the junior classes."

Changes came to South Union too. In 1910 "William Bates, Sabrina Whitmore, and Elizabeth Simmons all went to Auburn in a surrey to get things for Christmas, such as cheese, oranges, bananas, candies, mixed nuts, celery, 3 cans of green peas, and 2 bottles of green pickles."

When special days of national observance were proclaimed by the president, the nonpolitical Shakers always honored the request. One such day came during the 1849 cholera scourge when President Zachary Taylor recommended a day of humiliation, fasting, and prayer.

A different attitude, however, was taken toward election days. "November, 1888. Presidential election today. Who cares. Let them have their fight. We have a different warfare."

Although work and worship were religious counterparts in the Shaker mind, it was the usual practice to observe the biblical day of rest. There were times, however, when it was thought necessary to "bend the Sabbath" for practical reasons. "July 12, 1835. <u>Flax lifting Sabbath Infringement</u>. The brethren turned out this Sabbath day and lifted, bound, and hauled in 3 acres of flax. The excuse for this breach is that the flax is sufficiently retted and should rain fall on Monday, the crop would be ruined."

Other days, such as Christmas, might be bent also. Such was the case in 1867 at Pleasant Hill. Just when they were ready for the 1 P.M. Christmas service, a steamboat came up to the Shaker ferry for the first time that winter. The meeting was canceled immediately so the brethren could haul their freight down to the boat for shipping. "We made a donation to the poor and sent $300 to the Believers in Sweden," the account of the day's activities concluded.

On Christmas Day in 1856 all Pleasant Hill meetings were held, but the day ended with the brothers going out after supper to take ice out of the west pond to have it dry and ready for hauling the next morning.

To all Shakers, putting their hands to work was giving their hearts to God. They understood that a complete surrender meant a dedication of themselves, their time, their talents, and their property for the mutual support and benefit of other society members as well as for relief of those who were in need.

4

BEARING A SOUND,
GOOD CROSS

Soon after Mother Ann's Kentucky children began their Shaker experiment at Pleasant Hill and at South Union, they were to know trouble and to encounter problems. The incendiary burning of a barn filled with the autumn harvest, the destruction of a young orchard, denial of the right to speak in public, and harassment by mobs—these were some of the problems to be faced.

There were also times in the early years when little or no money was available. In 1810 a Pleasant Hill trustee had to swap "15 buttons off his old blue coat for 3 papers of common pins and 1 of large pins and ½ dozen needles."

As they began to overcome their economic problems, the Shakers found themselves faced with the growing opposition of their fellow citizens. The Kentucky legislature passed two laws designed to weaken the societies. These laws challenging the validity of the church covenant opened up a series of court cases.

The first law, passed in 1812, permitted divorce on the grounds that either the husband or the wife was joining the Shakers. The spouse not joining would receive all the property and all the children.

South Union became involved in a prolonged divorce suit

brought by Sally Boler against her husband, William, who had joined the society in 1808.

The case was dragged through both Barren and Logan county courts. Emotion ran high. Among the many depositions taken was one in which a woman stated that John Rankin, the preacher-leader, threw unwanted babies into the fire. This testimony was discounted.

Before a court decision could be reached, Boler deeded the land to the South Union trustees and fled with Daniel, his son, to live in an eastern society where Daniel grew up to become a leading Shaker elder.

A Pleasant Hill case that attracted widespread attention centered around Samuel Banta, one of the first Believers in Kentucky. After years of being a respected covenant member, Banta left the faith in the spring of 1827. He claimed that the society owed him approximately $4,000 for the money and property he had brought to the church.

Other apostates joined with Banta in a suit to break the Shaker covenant. The suit brought in the names of Gass and Banta commenced before Judge Kelly of the Mercer County Court but was removed to the Lincoln County Circuit Court under Judge Briggs, who decided against the apostates. Costs were then paid by the plaintiffs, who moved the suit on to the Kentucky Court of Appeals where it pended three years.

The legal adviser to the apostates seized upon the case as a means of getting elected to the state legislature. He began making inflammatory speeches in which he promised to get legislation passed that would compel the Shaker trustees to surrender or pay for all property brought by the departing member whenever application might be made. Furthermore it would provide for apostates to be paid for the time and services they had given the society.

For once, a campaign promise became a reality, and on February 11, 1828, the second law was passed that was expected to break up the Shakers and to deprive them of the means of defense in court. Both societies were soon beset not only by the suits of apostates but also by those brought by non-Shakers, who as heirs hoped to regain their family lands.

The Kentucky ministry began a countermovement by calling on Richard McNemar from Ohio to help get the two "obnoxious laws" repealed. He obliged by writing five "little blue books" with Pleasant Hill paying the publication costs.

Best known of the pamphlets were the *Investigator*, published in Lexington in 1828, and a shorter *Memorial* published in Harrodsburg under the joint signatures of John R. Bryant of Pleasant Hill and Eli McLean of South Union—both trustees. All the pamphlets were addressed to "the citizens of Kentucky in general and in particular to the Legislative and Executive departments of the state."

On December 13, 1830, Elder Benjamin and William Ligier left South Union to join the Pleasant Hill men in Frankfort. There they worked "in conjunction with Elder Eleazar [Richard McNemar], John Breathitt and J. T. Morehead, and some other friends to have certain statutes concerning Shakers repealed or so amended that they will not be injurious to us as a sect."

The bill had already been placed before the house by Morehead, a longtime acquaintance of South Union. In January, Pleasant Hill's neighbor Robert Wickliffe of Fayette County would speak in support of the bill in the senate. The speech was prepared by McNemar. But prejudice again won the day and the bill failed, even though many Kentucky judges had always considered the law unconstitutional.

Time passed and tensions lessened, but they did not completely disappear. The Shakers considered it fortunate that John Breathitt became governor in September 1832 and that he was succeeded by James T. Morehead.

The South Union leaders were also warmed by a letter from J. J. Crittenden in which he wrote regarding the *Gass-Banta* v. *Wilhite* case: "You may rely on my best services in it—stimulated by motives of personal kindness and friendship not less than by a sense of professional duty—I argued this case and it remains under the consideration of the judges till the next time."

While the apostates were waiting for the final court decision, they continued to demonstrate their animosity in many ways. For example, James Gass led a group to take over the Pleasant Hill gristmill. The day-long confrontation consisted of "little talking—just sitting." Later it was discovered that some among the group had pulled down portions of the Shaker fences.

A decision sustaining the church covenant was finally handed down by the appellate court on May 5, 1834. In June, Samuel Turner was delighted to report to New Lebanon: "We have now no concern with any suit at law and trust. We may never again have any, especially of the kind which has been so frequently and unjustly preferred against us—and which has caused so much trouble and annoyance, the principle of our covenant being now sufficiently recognized by the courts of justice to defeat their intention if not to bar them effectually."

Turner believed that the covenant had been put to a severer test in Kentucky than anywhere else the Believers had settled. He thought it significant that some heirs who were bringing a suit to recover a bequest to a Lexington Baptist church backed down after they learned of the court decision favoring the Shakers.

However irritating and discouraging these early reverses may have been, they faded in intensity when compared to those that evolved during the Civil War and the subsequent Reconstruction. Both societies felt the crosscurrents and tensions of the border territory where neighbors and even families were divided. Such a climate made it very difficult for the Shakers to sustain themselves as a neutral community. Their Federal neighbors reasoned that if the Shakers were abolitionists, they were for the United States government and would, of course, bear arms to support that same government. They could not understand the Shakers' pacifist position. On the other hand, Secessionist neighbors were intolerant of the Shakers, who had begun freeing their slaves as early as 1819. Thus the Shakers were suspect to both sides.

Of the two societies South Union found itself in the greater dilemma, because of its geographic location. Running through the very heart of the village was the state road connecting the towns of Bowling Green and Russellville—Bowling Green with its military forts and Russellville where the provisional government of the Kentucky Confederacy had been organized.

This same road led southwest beyond Russellville to Forts Donelson and Henry. Just west of South Union a second road intersected the Bowling Green-Russellville one. This road was the main artery to Green River and then on to the Ohio. Few roads in Kentucky carried more troop movement than these two, particularly in the early part of the war.

Skirting the southern edge of the South Union village and dividing the Shaker farm lands was the new Memphis branch of the Louisville and Nashville Railroad. And for the first time in American military history, the railroads were to help determine army routes.

Pleasant Hill, in the central part of the state and close to the regular seat of state government, was in a section less sharply divided in its civil and political principles. Although the Pleasant Hill Shakers had Southern sympathizers and supporters as neighbors, they had more who were Union or Federal in loyalty.

August 1, 1861, brought Pleasant Hill a foretaste of what lay ahead. On that day the journalist wrote: "Soldiers, called home guards, passed through this village today and mustered in the street. They are training and drilling and trying to learn the most successful methods of letting out the heart's blood of their opponents. . . . It is doubtful whether any of them on either side are able to tell why they are thus furiously seeking the lives of others."

Two weeks later the first "speck of war" was seen at South Union, and that speck was the arrival of Nathan Bedford Forrest with a company of 86 cavalrymen on their way to Camp Boone for training.

After a night's camping at the Shaker millpond, Forrest "called the men forward and told all who wished to return to their home to step out—that now was their last chance. Whereupon six left the ranks—who were then abused by him in language not suitable for our pen to record." The Shakers were shocked not only by the abusive language but also by the fact the men had spent the night "on the hard ground with nothing but the blue canopy for covering."

By the middle of September when the Confederates were occupying the Bowling Green forts, the South Union society found itself in the seceding part of Kentucky.

Each day held its reminder that the Logan County Shakers were "Way down in Dixie." One day agents came from Bowling Green commanding the brethren to furnish wagons and teams at the Rebels' set price. Other days blanket cloth was stolen out of the fulling mill; and still another day brought John C. Breckinridge's brigade of 5,000 men and 1,000 horses to fill the village road for two hours as they passed through on their way to Russellville "to protect the legislature assembled to form a provisional government."

The South Union leaders were well aware that if Kentucky seceded from the Union, their property would probably be confiscated and they would be forced to leave the state. As early as 1855 there had been a concerted effort on the part of some of their slave-holding neighbors "to exterminate the Shakers and drive them away to the North and then to seize and divide their property." It was even decided which individuals would be given the different Shaker houses.

The leader in this enterprise had been a Dr. Rhea, whose animosity had been inflamed when the Shaker trustees had outsmarted him in a land purchase. June 1 was the day set for the gathering of the mob and a meeting with the Shaker trustees, who arrived at the appointed site accompanied by a number of their friendly neighbors and by two attorneys, Lawyer Bristow of Elkton, who had been engaged by the society, and young Benjamin Grider of Bowling Green, who had volunteered his legal services.

John Burnam, a Bowling Green merchant who later would become the treasurer of the Kentucky Confederacy, was in the chair. When Bristow asked to speak, Burnam had polled the crowd expecting the vote to go against the Shakers. But Bristow won the majority vote, and spoke, appealing to those who "considered themselves law-abiding citizens and urging a legal and not an illegal course be pursued." He argued that if the Shakers had violated any law they should be prosecuted and "legally tried and punished, and if they had not, then those disturbing them would lay themselves liable to indictment and prosecution." Later, when the vote was taken, those in favor of mobbing the Shakers lost.

Though no further action was taken, feelings continued to run high. The following September when Trustee Eli McLean and Dr. Rhea chanced to meet out in the country, Rhea came up behind Eli's buggy and struck a blow on his head that laid Eli senseless for a moment. Fearing he had killed the man, "the doctor got water and bathed him and took the buggy and conveyed him to where some of the Brethren were at work . . . saying he found Eli in that condition and did not know by what means it came about. So he added sin to sin by lying about it." After many weeks of suffering, Eli recovered.

The ensuing years had not lessened the tensions, and so the Logan County Shakers had real reason to be concerned over the probable forming of a provisional state government that would be under Secessionist control.

As the war expanded and the Federals as well as the Confederates began to move throughout Kentucky, the Shakers of both colonies were actually to be victimized by their own reputation of being a generous and charitable people who, in accordance with their millennial law, never turned anyone away who needed help. It didn't take the soldiers long to learn that the Shaker villages were places where there were fruit-laden orchards and melon patches, where there was plenty of home-cooked food, and where one could get well-made cloth or perhaps a good fresh horse.

By late 1861, the troop movements through South Union had become fairly regular. For example: "Dec. 9. Captain Taylor came early in the morning and called for breakfast to be ready by eight o'clock for 250 cavalry. As usual we united two families and cooked breakfast for them." Only ten days later: "The Southern Pickets rode up about seven o'clock at night and called for supper for 400 soldiers. We were to have it ready by 8. We told them we were unable to cook for so many in so short a time. As it happened they got there not at 8 but at midnight and there were not 400 but 500."

One night after one o'clock the South Union sisters baked 600 pounds of bread. No wonder several of the South Union ovens had to be replaced during the war years.

The full menus are often listed. Breakfast might be:

> eggs
> sausage
> onions
> pickles
> as much milk as desired
> stewed apples
> butter and cornbread
> sassafras and sage tea (which the soldiers
>   jocosely called Jeff Davis coffee)

Another menu reads:

> good fresh coffee
> fresh loaf and biscuits
> boiled beef
> fried ham
> sweet and Irish potatoes
> 3 gal. can of green peaches
> fresh strawberries
> butter and cornbread and fried eggs

One officer on leaving the dinner table said to Sister Hannah, "Madam, I fear you will kill us with good vittles." Hannah replied, "Better that, than with a bullet."

The troop trains ran very close to the East family dwelling house. In her diary Eldress Nancy wrote: "The cars were so heavily laden the soldiers had to get out until the engine had ascended the grade; while labouring on, they would send forth most thundering cheers or hideous yells. Sometimes they were answered by soldiers camping in the village."

The large wave of military visits to Pleasant Hill did not begin until August 1862, but they continued very regularly during the next two months, being associated with an invasion of Kentucky by the Rebel officer John Hunt Morgan and with the coming battle of Perryville. "August 17. A company of U.S. cavalry encamped in our pasture below the East barn. We gave them supper and breakfast in the office yard and fed the horses at the cowpit. Also gave them lunch when they left at noon being ordered back to Harrodsburg." The next group was Confederate: "Sept. 3. A whole company, about one hundred of Morgan's followers . . . called for supper which we furnished and they camped in our office lot and threw out pickets in all the roads and approaches so that we were completely hemmed in and guarded under the Southern Confederacy."

The troops grew more numerous and the visits more frequent, reaching a climax in October when the soldiers "came pouring in by the thousands. Our feeding them rose say from 300 to 1000 per day and night with thousands of others begging for a small bite to eat, declaring they were nearly starved. This state of things continued until the 11th when the waggon trains came pouring in. They numbered 1,030 with about 10,000 soldiers with them. They started through before breakfast, the last of them passing after dinner."

The next day was Sunday, but there was an early call for breakfast. So instead of attending "to the spiritual duties of the Sabbath" the Believers went to work waiting on the soldiers until late in the night. With Morgan's soldiers drawn up in battle array all day, the society was fearful there would be a battle in the village. During all this time, the sisters had a "temporary table in the office yard, which they kept constantly filled."

A comparable day had come earlier at South Union. Wagons—both baggage and artillery—had rumbled by all day and late into the night. The same day some 1,200 soldiers came and camped on the premises. Eldress Nancy wrote: "As we look out of our windows we see the western portion of our little village, to all appearances a barracks for soldiers. The fires blazing, the sparks flying in high winds, their shouting and wild cheering contrast strongly with the peaceful and quiet appearance which has always characterized this place."

It did not help to know that the fires were kept going with the Shakers' new rail fence. In closing her description of the extraordinary day, Nancy wrote: "It is now near nine o'clock P.M. The Brethren are away attending to the soldiers and we are all alone."

Two days later she wrote: "All our hand labor is pretty much suspended, and the greater number of us are engaged in service for the army. The Brethren are actively engaged in hauling wood and attending to the various calls for the soldiers. The sisters are cooking, baking, etc., trying to keep the house in some degree of order and decency."

Of constant concern to the Kentucky Shakers was the matter of the draft. Pleasant Hill was fairly safe because the regular state government excused the Believers from military service, and also the Bluegrass section had furnished its quota of soldiers by voluntary enlistment. However, several of those volunteers had been young Shakers, who had found the martial music and the flying colors more exciting than the Shaker work program.

But at South Union, the enrolling officer took the names of all the Shaker men who were of draft age, and handbills were posted ordering all male citizens who had not done so to take the oath of allegiance to the United States. Many appeals for exemption were made directly to the military authorities and to the Kentucky legislature. Finally in 1863 the South Union ministry sent a letter to President Lincoln. It was four and one-half months before the answer came, in the form of a telegram from Secretary of War Stanton.

To the Provost Marshall of Bowling Green

Sir: If there is any religious community within your district whose conscientious scruples adjure war or the payment of the commutation fee, you will parole them indefinitely still holding them subject to any demand from the authority there.

Only a month later three young South Union Shaker brothers were drafted. Two were later released, but the third was held for service.

While the war currents continued to swirl about them, the Shakers, particularly those at South Union, learned that there was little difference between the Rebels and the Federals. Writing once of a company of Federal cavalry, Nancy said: "These men were as unreasonable as the Rebels were. War imbrutes instead of refines." A Pleasant Hill journalist lamented, "Lord, what is man when left to himself?" He felt the war had produced a world of thieves and desperadoes.

But those who kept the records at both communities were sensitive to the needs of the common soldiers and wrote graphic accounts of the soldiers' plight.

They devoured the raw lettuce with avidity; they surrounded our wells like the locusts of Egypt . . . and they struggled with each other for water as if perishing with thirst.

. . . they thronged our kitchen doors . . . begging for bread like hungry wolves. We nearly emptied our pantries of their contents and they tore the loaves and pies into fragments, devouring them!

. . . the main body was ragged and greedy and dirty and some barefooted and looked more like the inhabitants of pandemonium than the beings on this earth.

In the early part of the war, the Kentucky Shakers made no charges for the food they served either army. They considered feeding the hungry to be an act of charity in keeping with their millennial law. And they felt also that it was an act of self-protection—that is, they believed they would save more by being kind and accommodating than they would lose. And it was true that on many occasions after being served "the soldiers behaved quietly and orderly and made no depredations, or they might play two handsome tunes, swing their hats, and cheer for the Shakers."

The Pleasant Hill society also found that the much-feared John Hunt Morgan respected them. "General Morgan informed us that he and his command had intended taking up lodging with us but that our generosity had induced him to move further on to avoid oppressing us. Two of the company attempted to press a horse a piece but a counter order from the General prevented."

In a converse situation when several wagons stopped and foraged corn, the comment was made, "These have never been in our village, or they may not have done so."

Even when pay was offered for food the Pleasant Hill Shakers declined, receiving no compensation. However, it is true that they sometimes, by their own admission, "set limits, serving only such as we can afford," and they said they were careful at mealtimes "not to ring either the big or the little bell, for fear of a rush from the multitudes of the famishing."

At the more molested South Union, however, the society members were finally forced to charge a nominal sum. The price generally asked was seventy-five cents per soldier for two meals and overnight accommodations, a reasonable rate considering the soaring war prices.

But the charge was hard to collect, and the South Union journals carry many such accounts as, "Received $1. for feeding six soldiers," and "Fed another group. Got only a quarter from one man." On another occasion the 120 soldiers said nothing about pay. Neither did the Shakers. So they "got nothing but thanky."

There was one commodity the soldiers desired that the Shakers did not wish either to give or to sell—and that was horses. Both societies secreted their best horses in the woods or sent them out of the state, keeping only those that they had to have—and their oldest ones at that. Once the Pleasant Hill society joined neighbors in what was called "a stampede of mules and horses to escape Rebel clutches."

It was a common sight at both villages to see the marauders parade the streets demanding horses and traversing the pastures and fields in search of them. There are many entries such as, "Joseph Chalmers took a horse by violence," and "Two East house garden horses were stolen last night—Charley and Snap. Loss about $250.00."

At South Union an elder commented, "Generals Johnston and Buckner sent their agents to take our horses and wagons by force . . . but they delicately term it *pressing*." Someone else quipped that *steal* had become an obsolete word—that *press* and *appropriate* were now used in its stead.

The time came in January 1865 when South Union had so few horses left that in order to farm, they had to buy some mules from a neighbor. "We are driven to it of necessity," explained the elder, apologizing for breaking the Shaker rule of no mules.

An early Confederate order to Pleasant Hill had demanded that seven two-horse wagons be brought to Lexington. The brethren got back home with one of the wagons and $640 in Southern scrip.

Payments came not only in Southern scrip but also in receipts drawn upon the United States government. Neither was the Shakers' idea of the "one thing needful." It was observed that the officers had a "knack at drawing up their receipts in a way to get around making an honest payment for such things as forage, horses, hospital supplies, etc."

Eldress Nancy commented on South Union's problem. "It seems without a chance, the officers will swindle us out of all that sugar. . . . we could have sold every pound of it at the depot and to our neighbors and got the money down."

It was further suggested that the sugar would not be used for the sick soldiers but for the officers' brandy.

Although Pleasant Hill asked no money for the food served to the military groups, the trustees did charge for the corn, firewood, horses, and other supplies "pressed" by the armies. But they too found it impossible to receive full value. They considered that they had suffered a 90 percent loss when they were given Confederate scrip in pay for 700 fence rails, 200 stacks of corn, and between 3,000 and 4,000 bushels of old corn, as well as for the preserves and sanitary supplies they had furnished the sick and wounded in Harrodsburg and Perryville.

Even after initiating their policy of charging for food, the South Union society continued to extend charity in many ways. "Oct. 14, 1862, Brother Jefferson went to Bowling Green with provisions to give the sick soldiers 80 pies, 9 loaves of bread, dried beef, etc." And then there was the time when the sisters of the North and Centre families helped serve a

70

New Year's dinner for the soldiers at one of the Bowling Green forts, sending baked turkeys and chickens, doughnuts, two gallons of their own apple butter, and homemade catsup. One soldier expressed his intention of sending a specimen of "the superior bread all the way to Ioway." Another to express appreciation was a medical officer in the Bowling Green military hospital who sent South Union a gift supply of coffee "already browned."

Of course Pleasant Hill went the extra mile too, carrying sanitary supplies and provisions to the sick and wounded soldiers in Harrodsburg, where there were six or seven hundred of the "fruits of Perryville."

The Shakers soon learned that they would be denounced almost as often as they would be blessed. Once a lieutenant who had failed to get a fresh horse called out angrily: "You ought to be blowed out and the place destroyed. Here we are going night and day to protect you and what in the name of Hell do you do for your country?"

Many other Kentuckians also felt that the Shakers were failing as citizens, that in dancing and singing, in planting and hoeing, in tending the silk worms, laying new walks, and setting out pine trees they were not contributing anything constructive to the war effort, but were instead continuing to prosper in spite of, if not because of, the national crisis.

The truth is that the noncombatant Shakers found the war years a time of danger and of greatly diminished prosperity. They might continue their wood cutting with a newly installed circular saw, but they found it expedient to post a sentry to warn them if they needed to flee with their horses. And while the brethren in both societies continued as best they could their annual farm work, they realized that they might be sowing clover for army mules—for "who shall eat the crops to be raised is beyond our ken."

Pleasant Hill reported to Union Village that the society's greatest loss was in the stagnation of all kinds of business and the blockade of the market. South Union suffered an indefinite delay of their 1862 spring seed order from Scotland. Their

71

merchant Dods wrote he could not ship for "want of freight," and he hoped there would be a favorable change in national affairs soon.

A report sent to the Union Village Shakers regarding affairs in Kentucky stated: "Every species of property is at ruinous low prices except articles for immediate consumption. Distrust has seized the mind of the people and nothing but money or food has any fixed value." The merchants found that brooms and seed, cloth and bonnets brought low prices when they could be sold at all; yet their own groceries and other household necessities had to be purchased at very high figures. A report sent from Pleasant Hill to New Lebanon in 1863 stated: "Financially we are very low. We do not support ourselves nor keep up repairs at present." One writer put it succinctly, saying they only "patched and propped to keep things on their legs."

Going to Lexington to sell strawberries, the Pleasant Hill merchants found a dull market "by reason of great excitement prevailing about General John Morgan having invaded the state."

Trips related to the war often interrupted the regular daily routines. For example, the Pleasant Hill brethren had to go to Frankfort to bring back their own ferryboats after the Federals carried them off to thwart the Confederates. The South Union trustees had to go to Russellville to give the Rebel government "the only two guns in the society." But when the Confederate officers learned that the society had only two guns for the use of so many people, they let the brethren "bring the most indifferent one back."

The full story of the four turbulent war years is one of rumors "as plenty as leaves in autumn" and of fears—some real, some baseless. At Pleasant Hill it was a time when the usual peaceful quiet was broken by the heavy tramp of the infantry and by gunfire resounding from the rugged Kentucky River cliffs. At South Union it was a period of petty annoyances, such as clouds of August dust stirred by the passing cavalry, rising as high as the houses, and wide-mouthed cannon wheeled within twenty paces of the family dwellings. Both societies experienced such inconveniences as irregular mails and no mails at all and such delays as Pleasant Hill's having to wait for the war's end to have a Cleveland dentist come to make and insert sixty-three teeth.

It was also a time of spiritual revelations, of inspirational hymns, and of messages from the spirits of departed Believers, experiences commonly related to periods of high emotion. "Mch. 1863—The weather is cloudy and spitting snow at intervals all day. I was reclining in a passive quiet position when the spirit of Mercy Dunn and another shadowy spirit behind Mercy asked the question 'What does it take to make a sound believer?' Mercy D. answered, 'One that don't flinch at crosses or troubles but <u>bears a sound good cross.</u>' " Such inspirational references appear as late as 1872.

Perhaps the heaviest of all the crosses was the tension resulting from the constant attempt "to remain neutral and calm, yet firm in their duty. To say but little on either side." Elder John Eads wrote Daniel Myrick, an eastern elder: "Our head was in the Lion's mouth. We had to be passive. Prudence would dictate nothing else." But Eads confided to his friend that "with many of us there is a very strong Southern sympathy existing. Our habits of life being a good deal Southern, including in some degree the slavery sense . . . doing all our trading in the South and getting our temporal income from that direction." It was, indeed, a lonely and precarious position "the two little handfuls of Shakers" attempted to hold in the border state of Kentucky.

The Reconstruction period did not bring an end to the problems. It was a time when the Kentucky societies were made up of "the very old and the very young with a kind of gap or hiatus that wants fixing up between them."

The trustees in both societies began hiring blacks to take up the work slack. For example, in 1867 South Union arranged for twenty "hirelings" to be assigned to the various shops and the farm. To keep the sisters from having to do the extra cooking, the trustees gave the blacks permission to erect family cabins on the Shaker land. In addition to his housing, each hireling was to receive a yearly allotment of 500 pounds of pork and enough meal for his standard diet of "corn dodgers and bacon." He was also to receive $125 in annual wages.

The first cabin erected for the hirelings was torn down in the night, before it could be occupied. A second one was torn down before it was finished.

A notice addressed to Urban Johns was found pinned to a sugar maple in the West family yard. "We invite you to bring your Negroes into your enclosure. If you do not we will <u>Bushwhack</u> you. We want to bust your noggan in anyhow. You had better stay clost. Signed, Regulators. Logan Co., Ky."

In his journal account of the incident, Harvey Eades (as this member of the family usually spelled it) commented that it was the "last kicking of the old devil who wanted to drive out the Shakers in 1855. Then they owned the Negro, now they can't even hire him and are mad because the Shakers can."

Pleasant Hill found similar threats tacked on their post office door. Couched in vulgar language the notes were warnings to dismiss the hired Negroes or the blacks would be driven or burned out.

It happened that during the same period when the need for more able-bodied men was critical, the Pleasant Hill trustees heard that a number of new Swedish Believers wished to emigrate to the United States but were too poor to pay their own passage.

The society leaders felt an obligation to help the Swedes, but they also recognized a chance to add men to the society work force. So chiefly between 1867 and 1871 "pecuniary aid" was furnished for the removal of these Believers to Pleasant Hill. Andrew Bloomberg, who had been a Pleasant Hill member for some years, began taking the lead in helping his compatriots come to Kentucky. Upon arrival the Swedes were formed into the West Lot family with Bloomberg as their family leader.

The lack of manpower was not the only problem during the days of Reconstruction. Robberies continued to be frequent. Pleasant Hill experienced a midnight robbery when six men "flintered the post office door" with a block of stone from the steps. Angered when they found very little money, they capsized the letterpress. Next day they surrounded the brick office intending to have Bryant, the trustee, "deliver the contents of the coffers." But Bryant went out a back door and made a run for the Centre House where the alarm bell was sounded. The robbers left, "firing a volley at every moving object and at some of the buildings."

As late as August 1874, South Union was complaining: "We are still annoyed with the wicked who are always on the alert to do us harm. They are daily prowling through our vineyards and orchards stealing fruit by the meal sack full . . . made opening in window sash of mill house—and took what grain they could."

Worst of all were the incendiary fires which became almost commonplace at both South Union and Pleasant Hill. The first of the disastrous postwar fires was at South Union in September 1868. The black hirelings had told the trustees a few days earlier that the mills were to be burned, but having heard "the wolf cry" so often the leaders paid little attention. At the time of the fire no alarm was given by either the hired spinner or hired miller, both of whom lived in houses adjacent to the mills. Although these men were both to be dismissed in a few weeks, they were not suspected of the arson. However, it was almost certain that they knew about the plot.

It was not until the rising bell sounded that the villagers knew their loss at the mill dam. The fire completely consumed the two three-story buildings—the 100-foot-long woolen mill and the 75-by-45–foot gristmill—which were connected by a bridge. The loss of the buildings and their contents was estimated to be between $60,000 and $75,000.

An appeal was made to Governor John Stevenson to extend protection and to offer a reward, but no special action was ever taken by the governor. Little wonder that one journalist felt that "Kentucky at this time is the worst state in or out of the Union, and we seem to be in the worst part of it."

The loss was a bitter one, because it had been less than a year since the society had added the third story to the woolen factory and filled the building with machinery, including a 45-horsepower steam engine to be used in running both the woolen mill and the gristmill. At a time of high prices, the outlay had been "not less than $25,000."

The ministry determined to rebuild the gristmill at once. Only seventeen months later, the mill was in operation, becoming once again the source of considerable income. Shipments of flour could be made by railroad now that the war was over.

The woolen mill, however, was not replaced, because for some time it had been running "on *half force* and *whole expense*." When the hired foreman had not been "able to get up the Indigo blue dye," the sisters had been asked to take over the coloring. Soon they had to take over the looms, where they tried to increase the production of the weaving, "mostly jeans, blankets and cashmere."

Even before the fire, the leaders had begun to understand that the new machine age was to bring the Shaker industries very strong competition. Not replacing the woolen mill appears to have been a practical decision.

The incendiary fires at Pleasant Hill were neither so numerous nor so disastrous as those at South Union. But in 1876 a large stock barn, along with a dozen little surrounding buildings, was set fire. Lost also were thirty pairs of harness, carriages, and grain. Another of the incendiary fires occurred in 1891 when the bridge over Shawnee Run, near the millpond, was burned.

The leaders in each society were shocked to have fires set by one of their own young people. In August 1873, young Rodney Bloomberg, son of Peter Bloomberg, one of the leaders of the West Lot family, set fire to the North family cow-barn with all its contents. The stone walls were too shattered to be repaired.

At South Union it was a rebellious young sister who, early one April morning in 1871, set fire to the Centre House garret. Through hard work and luck the fire was extinguished, but the charred garret timbers remain today as a reminder of the lawlessness and disharmony that followed the civil conflict.

Rodney and the young sister exemplified the rebellious spirit that was not only abroad in the state but was being felt by the young Shakers who resented the leadership of a ministry that had governed too long. Indeed Elder Eades had been perceptive when he observed that there was a gap or a hiatus that needed "fixing up" between the very old and the very young.

In both societies the ministry worked as zealously to revive the spiritual conditions as the trustees did to revitalize the economic conditions. But something had gone out of many of the hearts, and many of the hands now faltered.

The promise of utopian living which had seemed so near in the late forties and early fifties was never to be fulfilled in Kentucky. The war years and the subsequent Reconstruction period contributed heavily to the decline which finally brought the closing of Pleasant Hill in 1910 and of South Union in 1922.

5

THE ENDING OF
SHAKERISM
IN KENTUCKY

THE LAST FIFTY YEARS of Shakerism in Kentucky (1872–1922) were full of change.

Gone were the years when the work was directed by eastern leaders. By 1841 the last of the veterans had either returned to one of the eastern societies or had been buried in Kentucky or Ohio.

The Pleasant Hill journal entry for May 9, 1835, records one of several homegoings. "Eldress Hopewell Curtice set out for New Lebanon to return no more, having filled a lot in the ministry at Pleasant Hill ever since June 5, 1809. She went by way of Louisville where she was joined by Eldress Mercy Pickett of South Union and thence through Ohio where Elder Issacher Bates, then residing at WaterVliet, joined the company—all of whom were returning home to New Lebanon there to abide."

One who did not return east was Molly Goodrich of South Union, who died in December after Mercy had left in May. Molly had come west in 1806 and had been in the South Union ministry since 1811.

At the late afternoon burial, the sorrowful company sang a hymn composed in Molly's honor. It ended:

Strip'd. Bereaved of our blest Mother
From whose bosom we've been fed,
How can we our sorrow smother
That she's numbered with the dead.

Now that both eldresses were gone, Molly to "heaven above" and Mercy to her "heavenly home at New Lebanon," Elder Benjamin said he felt like a "father left with a house full of motherless children." Adding to his loneliness was his awareness that of the eastern leaders only he and Anna Cole of Pleasant Hill remained in the so-called western territory.

By October of the following year, Benjamin too announced his resignation as "a minister and lead" to South Union and began to pack his articles and notions for his trip home. Before leaving he received a letter from his "old friend Joel," who wrote on behalf of the Pleasant Hill ministry thanking him for his part in bringing "the seeds of Mother's gospel amongst us."

Eighteen years later in 1854 the new South Union ministry visited New Lebanon and spent some happy hours with the eighty-one-year-old Benjamin, who doubtless had many questions to ask about South Union and Pleasant Hill. He expressed a wish that the visitors would take home some things which he said "properly belonged to South Union." Among the articles he packed into "two little trunkfuls" were several journals he had written and "many little accts. of matters and things pertaining to his journeys in the West." He gave a parting blessing and greatly desired the prosperity of the South Union society.

After thirty-four years at Pleasant Hill, Anna Cole returned east in June 1841. She was said to have been a "Mother in Israel, a bright example of truth, justice, and tender care."

By the end of the 1860s the Kentucky societies had lost not only their first leaders but also most of their pioneer members. Among those who died at Pleasant Hill were three who had joined the first year.

Jan. 3, 1856. Molly Banta deceased—being 78 years of age, had set out in February, 1806, and had stood through many trying scenes where many had fallen.

Mch. 1856. Anthony Dunlavy—deceased of an inveterate cancer— being in his 84th year. Had embraced the faith in 1806.

Mch. 6, 1856. Cassia Dunlavy—breathed her last in her 88th year the 26th of last October. She was the first of any in Kentucky who embraced the gospel in the West Country and has been a faithful and unblemished pillar in the church ever since.

Most of the early Believers at South Union died during the same period. One who would be sorely missed was John Rankin, Sr., who died July 12, 1850, at ninety-two. As a minister of the Presbyterian church, Rankin had been the first man in the Gasper territory to open his home and his church to the three Shaker missionaries. Receiving the testimony along with his helpmate, Rebecca, Rankin had given his brick house and land to be used by the beginning Gasper society. Of the ten Rankin children all had become important Believers "except Robert, who turned back."

Rankin was always admired for his unusual physical strength and energy. It was recorded that he worked hard when he was seventy and eighty, doing "a great deal both spiritual and temporal."

There were also William Rice (d. 1863), the chief singer in the society for forty years, and Samuel Robinson (d. 1854), who had a "cool, philosophic make of mind." Robinson, the victim of an enlarged liver, "desired to have his body opened" to see whether any information could be found by the operation.

The American life expectancy in the 1850s was forty years, whereas the average age at death of Molly, Anthony, and Samuel was eighty-two. Longevity has always been a marked characteristic of the American Shakers.

Throughout the 1840s the second-generation Shakers gradually replaced the earliest Believers in the roles of leadership. Most of the new leaders had come as children with their parents to South Union. The familiar names that continued to be written into the society chronicles were Rankin and Johns, McComb and McLean, Eads or Eades, as well as Houston, Shannon, and Moore. At Pleasant Hill the story was much the same.

The new leadership came during the most normal period the Kentucky Shakers were ever to experience. The organization days marked by hardship had passed. The large building program was nearing completion. The cleared land was yielding good crops, and the industrial program was returning considerable profit.

But the years passed and the joys of ordered living gave way to the distress and lawlessness of the Civil War and Reconstruction and to the complexities of the machine age and growing urbanization. By the 1870s the communities began to show signs of an imminent decline.

The threatened decline was one reason the South Union trustees renewed their efforts to bring in orphan children. Although the leaders hoped the children would eventually become members, they knew from past experience that very few would ever sign the covenant.

An 1867 journal entry contains a familiar story.

Gone at last! Achille L'Hotte left clandestinely today, being the last one of a lot of eighteen boys brought from the orphan asylum at New Orleans on the 5th of January, 1843. One very good and promising youth and two others untried died here. All the rest, some earlier, chose the world. Achille, the last to go, is 34 years old. The oldest of the lot was only 12 years of age, the youngest 8. They are all gone and vanished out of sight in 24 years. It becomes a question whether we are doing the best we can, or as we should, in taking in destitute children. Certainly there cannot be much gain if not one in 20 remains true to the good cause. We now have between 30 or 40. Shall not one be saved?

In spite of Eades's doubts the society continued to take needy children. Not all came as orphans, for some were accompanied by their war-widowed mothers. Others were brought by their poverty-stricken parents to be apprenticed to the society.

It was said by some outsiders that "rather than have no children the Shakers would take bad children." No doubt there were some problem children among the orphans. But the society was protected against keeping incorrigible children whose parents had left them to be educated and taught a trade. The indenture papers made it clear that children would be kept only if they could learn and were manageable. Also the arrangement held only on the condition the Shakers liked the children and the children liked the Shakers.

The program for the children was not all study and work. To relieve any homesickness or to erase unhappy war memories, there were outings to pick berries or gather hickory nuts, to fish, and to picnic in the woods. That the children enjoyed the outdoor activity is reflected in a school composition by little Alice Montgomery of Pleasant Hill, "In the spring I love to go down on the cliffs which are very pretty, so many colors togeather. I can see the river, it looks like it is standing still. Yet I know it is running as fast as it can into another river which runs to the ocean." Between 1865 and 1870 the children's recreational activities were greatly increased.

An official effort to offset the economic and spiritual decline among the Kentucky Shakers was a plan announced in October 1868 by the "fountain head in the East." It was a plan whereby Pleasant Hill and South Union were to be formed into one bishopric and be governed by a joint ministry. It was believed this action would strengthen both.

Appointed to the joint ministry were James Rankin and Pauline Bryant of Pleasant Hill and Harvey Eades and Betsy Smith of South Union. The ministry was in residence chiefly at South Union, but from time to time spent several weeks on "the hill" in Mercer County. "Journey Ministry. We set out for Pleasant Hill this morning. Will stop at Lebanon Junction and arrive there tomorrow, the Lord willing."

The time needed to travel 130 miles between the villages was a deterrent to a successful joint ministry, and in June 1872 the plan was discontinued, having been in operation a little less than four years—October 1868–June 1872.

Returning to Pleasant Hill, Rankin again stood first in the society until 1874 when he became eighty-two; he was then replaced by B. B. Dunlavy, who was already seventy. At the same time Thomas Shain, who was already eighty-two, was appointed elder in the Centre family.

In recording these appointments in the South Union journal, Harvey Eades commented: "Old Battle Scarred Veterans, why don't you all resign—and simply hold up and support some younger men—How silly all this seems to be to this writer—I may also be so foolish when I arrive at this age."

Ten years later Eades inserted a note into the 1874 entry, saying, "I am just that foolish now. Nearly 78 and cannot find anyone to take my place yet—sorry I am." When Eades died in his eighty-seventh year, he was serving both as elder and as trustee.

The leaders at both South Union and Pleasant Hill were discouraged by the lack of members who were either capable or desirous of assuming leadership. They were also alarmed that the departure of members far exceeded the arrivals.

At the time the joint ministry had been installed, the combined membership of Kentucky Shakers was 673. Three years later the total had fallen to 497. By June 1881 it was reported that the membership of Union Village, Ohio, which once numbered 700, had dropped to 137, and of these there were scarcely any substantial Shakers aside from "the aged first born." Pleasant Hill, once "between 4 and 500 souls, had about 160," and South Union was reduced from its peak of 350 members to 215, but 30 of this number were children.

It was also a matter of great concern that by 1881 both Union Village and Pleasant Hill were in debt, "the former about $6,000 and the latter . . . some $14,000." It was hoped that with "their good lands and buildings they would soon pay their way out." But at South Union, Eades added, "We at this writing are clear of debt and have a few thousand."

Although South Union had no debts, its bank savings had been greatly reduced in 1870 when a Bowling Green cashier absconded with funds including gold lumps and $80,000 in bank notes that South Union had placed in the bank's deposit vault. Finally after "considerable trouble Urban Johns, trustee, found 36 of the $1,000 bonds in New York where they had been placed on the market." After the bank suit had been compromised, the total loss of the notes and gold was estimated at $63,000.

To bolster their working cash funds, the leaders decided to sell the society "out farms." The forty-acre fruit farm, Canaan, was sold in 1876 for $1,200 and the remaining remnant of the Black Lick Farm was sold in 1885 to J. B. Winston for $5,000.

Economic conditions grew worse for both Pleasant Hill and South Union because of the national financial panic of 1873, the increasing competition from the new commercial processes, the cost of more hired workers, and the mounting expense of taking the produce and cattle to market. For example, the annual profit from all South Union industries in 1884 did not quite reach $4,000.

Hoping to stimulate business, Elder Eades began in the 1880s to publish an annual farm catalog. The 1885 issue, containing 32 pages, was addressed to friends and patrons. It set forth detailed information about the garden seeds, plants (such as sweet potato, tomato, and strawberry), and onion sets, which could be ordered. Also described were preserves and jellies, brooms, and livestock. Several pages were devoted to the purebred poultry the Shakers raised by then. Among the breeds described were Light Brahmas, Patridge Cochins, Brown Leghorns, and Wyandottes. Available also were Imperial Pekin ducks, Mammoth Bronze turkeys, and Speckled guineas. Fowls or clutches of eggs could be shipped by express. Eldress Jane Cowan was in charge of the poultry business for many years.

But such brave new ventures as a newly designed commercial catalog had little effect on the shrinking markets.

Pleasant Hill's major income continued to be from cattle. But they too had a poultry industry under the management of Susan Murray. Also the brothers were experimenting with the raising of Italian bees.

With the national shift from agriculture to industry, the younger Shakers were attracted to the cities where paid factory employment could be obtained. The older, but still able-bodied men were being drawn to the free government lands in the new West where they hoped to turn their farming skills to their own profit. As a result, the society memberships continued to dwindle.

The decline, however, was not peculiar to the Shaker societies, for other communal groups were either breaking up or had already dissolved. Nineteenth-century utopianism was no longer the exciting elixir it once had been. There were still some people who wished to be admitted to the Shaker villages, but most were looking for comfort and security, not for an opportunity to work and worship. At the turn of the twentieth century a new Shaker law had to be enacted requiring all applicants to have healthy bodies and to be under fifty years of age.

As much as they longed for additional members, the leaders found it prudent to refuse many applicants. For example, "an aged man came seeking a home but was not admitted. And there was also a widow with two children who wished a home with us, but will not be admitted."

It had not been long since another woman and her children had been accepted. But a short time later she had left with a man who came claiming she was his wife. It was noted that "they took great care to slip away without the children." Nettie Lyle also slipped off leaving her children in the Shakers' care, but it was not for long; the elder sent the children back to her.

Pleasant Hill and South Union began taking boarders. But the new policy seems to have been as much to erase the lonely appearance of the villages as it was to increase the society income. In January 1873, at South Union, "Samuel Gilmore entered into an agreement to $50 per year for the support of his mother." But in November when Samuel returned for a visit, he was encouraged to take her away. No money was ever to be received from the Gilmores.

From 1880 on, it became necessary to expel members because of their rebellious spirit or disorderly conduct.

1880. Sent Away. Martin Lafollet thinks he might as well have a wife as anybody.

March 8,1880. A Fuss. Had trouble yesterday getting rid of the Ed Stanwick family from Kansas. Had to forcibly put the woman out in the street. She then got into the wagon and was driven away.

Oct., 1886. T. M. McRae is advised to go. After 18 or 19 years of struggle can't come into covenant—has never any more than been worth his board to society. This should be a lesson to others who only have one end of Christ's yoke on their shoulders.

The Pleasant Hill leaders did not seem to be as firm as those at South Union in confronting the obvious "Winter Shakers." Self-criticism is sometimes found in their journals: "We have hardly anything now to live on and yet we take in every tramp that comes along. They go at loose ends, do just as they please, & say what they choose & not half pay their board all winter—then leave in the spring with all we have in clothes & food."

But the elder who embezzled family funds was expelled. And some action must have been taken when it was learned that certain farm deacons and farm hands had been selling produce and keeping the money.

At South Union a new member got away with a team, a wagon, and $100 worth of brooms. He was caught and imprisoned. Another who collected $1,000 on a seed trip never returned to the village.

During the same period many other instances of unbecoming behavior had to be recorded in the society journals, such as, "George Spillman and Ella had words this morning," or "Frances went some place yesterday evening but wouldn't tell where."

Worst of all, South Union had its first murder. Charles Mayfort shot and killed William Horne at the North family dwelling. It was thought the trouble grew out of "jealousy about a girl who resided in the family."

Probably no act of defiance caused more talk in the village and among the neighborhood than Ida Ladd's marriage. "May 3, 1890. Married—Ida Ladd aged about 20 years went from the West family and was married at the Tavern at our Depot on Sabbath 1st instant. The first time in the history of South

Union that such a thing has occurred—It was brought about by advertising and secret letter writing and exchanging Photos."

Ida's wedding could be tolerated better than an earlier situation at Pleasant Hill. "December 5, 1883. Marion and Henry Scarball who have been living in the C[entre] F[amily] some years past got Denica Perkins & Sally Monday in a Family way between them this summer. This is the kind of Shakers we have now days." When Elder Dunlavy asked the young men to leave, they refused to go unless they received cash, Henry asking fifty dollars and Marion seventy. The journal comment was "This is awful."

Another shocking event took place at the South Union tavern when Richard Turner, an avowed enemy of the Shakers, elected to commit suicide there. It was in March 1889 that Squire Turner walked into the tavern and went to the washroom where he took a dose of morphine and whiskey and then killed himself.

Actions among some members as well as among the people around them bore out an elder's observation made in 1872 that "temporalities have the uppermost seat in the synagogue." Even the Sabbath day entries began to reflect the waning spiritual vitality.

Dec. 3, 1889—Labored one song in the dance, the little song "I'll be a David." There were only 7 Davids of masculine and 8 feminine. Rest stood around walls or sat on their seats.

Aug. 3, 1890. Society meeting. Sorrowful, pitiable sight. Few, say a half dozen grown sisters and one dozen children in the marching circle. All, or nearly so, dressed as worldly as possible. Can hardly be told as Shakers and a few brethren—only three men dressed in Shaker costume.

In 1889 when no meeting was held on the Savior's birthday in any branch of the South Union society, the ministry knew "the harps were on the willows and the sound of the grinding was low."

The Shakers began to attend outside services, going to a

Baptist protracted meeting or riding out to the Presbyterian Knob church. To help offset outside interests, a new music program was introduced in the form of a singing school. A special music room was opened and equipped with a new Chickering piano, hauled from Bowling Green, and six dozen new chairs ordered from Louisville. During the winter of 1873–1874 Brother Nicholas Briggs of Canterbury, New Hampshire, directed an intensive music program "to bring up the gift of singing."

The children, too, were to have a new educational experience, for in 1880 a coeducational school was tried for the first time at South Union. Sixty children were enrolled.

Although the journals covering the last fifty years of Kentucky Shakerism contain more entries pertaining to failure and disappointment than to the good Shaker life, there was, nevertheless, a continuing pattern of normal happenings. A new family dwelling was completed, an old building got a new slate roof, a cistern was dug, and the elder's room got a "very good but rather gaudy" new carpet. The women brought in willow for making baskets and gathered stramonium leaves for the medicinal herb market. The men went to Illinois, Missouri, and even to Texas with cattle to sell.

New machinery was tried out and purchased if it appeared it would be helpful. Added to the equipment were straw-cutting machines, seed separators, a wheat thresher, a gasoline plow, and a cross-cut saw that ran by turning a crank. At Pleasant Hill a new dumping wagon was invented by the society dentist, Francis Pennebaker. Models were made to sell, but sales were few.

Electric call bells and telephones were installed to be used between some buildings. In 1878 a stretch of macadamized road was built through the South Union village, costing $3,804. In 1881 windmills were erected at three of the South Union family dwellings.

Although the time had come when manufactured cloth was replacing home-woven textiles, the clothes were still made in the societies. However, the women now did the tailoring for the men. The summer sewing might be a vest for each man and "two dresses a piece for the sisters—one lawn and one print."

Some adjustments in the work schedule had to be made to accommodate an aging membership. "Dec. 11, 1871. A new arrangement. The aged sisters are required to attend to putting up the clothes on Monday morning. On Tuesday all who are able to assist with the ironing. No one is expected to go beyond their ability."

In 1872 it was announced that when the society services were held in the family meeting room, it would be permissible to take in their chairs to make themselves comfortable. A change was also made in the meals. To save both work and cost, the societies tried two meals a day—morning and noon—"saving a few crackers for supper." An adjustment made at South Union in 1909 was moving the dining tables into the kitchen during the severe winter months to save wood.

At Pleasant Hill the younger members were advocating changes that challenged Elder Dunlavy and the old order. Chief among the protesters were the Pennebaker brothers, William and Francis, who had grown up in the society although they had gone to Cincinnati for their professional training—William as a physician, Francis as a dentist. It was William who headed the West family after the group revolted against the ministry and declared itself an independent family.

On a visit to Pleasant Hill in 1884, Eldress Harriet Bullard noted that "not much of the Believer element" existed at the West family. She found that "they have things about their own way. Raise horses and have a race course. We cannot see how the blessing of God can attend such proceedings."

Death came to Dunlavy in 1886 and at the same time Eldress Pauline was near death, leaving the society as if it were headless. It was not until Dunlavy's death that it was discovered how inept his financial management had become. The society found itself encumbered with a large mortgage and some worthless shares of Nevada gold-mining stock. The total debt was $46,000.

The financial burden was too much for too few. In 1896 the

trustees finally arranged a $30,000 mortgage on 3,334 acres with the Louisville Title Company. They sold 766 acres and the Trustees' Office building to David Castleman of Louisville. The empty East family dwelling was rented to A. M. Barkley of Lexington, who began operating a hotel. He placed Sister Jane Sutton in charge.

Ironically the rebellious young West family, under the astute management of William Pennebaker, succeeded financially through land leases and diversified interests in livestock and farming. There were times, however, when Pennebaker had to borrow several hundred dollars from the First National Bank in Harrodsburg, probably to meet running expenses. Eventually, the West family was combined with the Centre and East groups.

Finally in September 1910 the inevitable came about. The twelve remaining Shakers deeded their 1,800 acres to George Bohon, with the agreement he would care for them until the end of their lives.

Among those remaining were Jane Sutton and John Pilkington who died within twenty-four hours of each other and were buried the last day of 1912. Their deaths left only Mary Settles, Susan Murray, and Sarah Nagle at the Centre dwelling. In reporting the deaths to South Union, William Pennebaker added, "My understanding is that the village people live off the money in the bank and produce from the farm." But the farm was to be managed by the new owner after the first of March, 1913.

Pennebaker died in 1922, the last of the Pleasant Hill brothers. Mary Settles, the last sister, died in 1923.

The year 1910 had brought not only the closing of Pleasant Hill but also the end of Union Village in Ohio. Four other western societies had closed even earlier, leaving the "outer branch of the vineyard," or South Union, as the sole branch of Shakerism in the West. Being so widely separated from the eastern ministry, Elder Logan Johns and Eldress Lucilla Booker must have had a deep sense of lost direction. They were also saddened by the knowledge that "the habits and customs of the Gentiles around them" were very much interwoven into the lives of the remaining society members.

The annual South Union census for 1911 showed only thirteen members—four at the office, three in the East house, and six at the Centre. The West family had been combined with the Centre twenty years earlier.

Of the thirteen, one was a boy, Risdon, who went to school in the nearby town of Auburn. The society had ten men hired by the month and two by the day. The store, the hotel, and the blacksmith shop located at the railroad station were leased.

The official journal was no longer filled with full daily accounts of the society's industries or of the spiritual life. Instead the daily accounts contained personal items such as, "Josie Bridges bought a new white metal bedstead for herself" or "Lizzie Simmons is having the 12th and 14th rooms cleaned today; both of them to be occupied by her—one to live in, the other for company." It became the practice for the sisters to have their room walls either papered or calcimined and to cover the earlier red and ochre milk stains with commercial paint. It became customary to tack down the carpet on the retiring room floors. Furniture was often varnished as part of the spring cleaning process.

Mirrors and pictures were now hung on the traditionally bare walls. Mary Wann hung the oil portraits of her Scottish parents and Frances Cary displayed some of her choice English china on the walls of their rooms.

There was still a communal treasury, but some members held on to private funds with which to satisfy their personal wants. An organ was purchased for the meeting room, but Josie Thrall bought herself a 1913 Victrola. The young ladies of the area loved to visit Miss Josie's room to hear the latest Victor records she had bought in Bowling Green.

The making of clothes was no longer strictly a communal activity. The trustees "Perryman and Carr went to Russellville to get their measures taken for suits of clothes." Josie Thrall went to Auburn to have Mrs. Romans do some dressmaking for her.

Eldress Lucilla sewed for herself, making two dress skirts, one of "flowered linen lawn" and the other of "waterproof" material. She also made two flowered red curtains for her window. Sewing materials were now bought at the South Union store or in the neighboring towns.

It seemed more in keeping with tradition when the eldress spent an afternoon "mending the blankets by cross stitching the ends." A few days later she was "choring," putting away the family blankets and comforts from moths.

A day's journal entry might simply recount that it was show day in Bowling Green and that Sister Sabrina Whitmore had gone in a surrey with neighbor Charlie Tatum, his wife, and her sister Mabel to attend the show. One October evening three sisters and a brother went to neighbor Guthrie Coke's house to a party.

Another time some of the brethren went to vote in the primary election for the governor of Kentucky. Voting in a political election signified a definite change in Shaker policy.

There were other changes. Carpet brushes were now bought, not made. Eggs, butter, and chickens were exchanged at the stores for light bread and other needed supplies. A tone of disapproval is noted in a 1913 entry recording the "first bought laundry soap." Beef was obtained not by slaughtering but by joining the Logan County beef club. In 1914 the little society made arrangements with a tenant for raising tobacco on the shares. This was a new crop for the South Union community, though Pleasant Hill had grown it in the early years.

The Shaker bent for being progressive did not desert the small handful of Logan County Shakers. In April 1915, the trustees paid a thousand dollars for a new "Lilly Rio" automobile. As soon as Will Bates learned to drive, there was hardly a day that the new automobile was not used to take somebody somewhere either on a business errand or on an outing for pleasure—to the area baseball games, for example, or to holiday celebrations.

In 1916 the trustees had two Russellville plumbers come to install "a bathroom and water closet" in two separate Centre

House rooms. As early as 1908 coal grates had been cut in the rooms which were occupied, thus replacing the little wood stoves that had been used since 1833. It had become easier to obtain coal than wood.

By 1910 a telephone with an outside line was installed so doctors could be called when needed. Not only was the society now dependent on outside physicians, but the local ministers often preached the funeral sermons. Coffins were now purchased rather than made. There had been a time when the world bought its coffins at Shakertown.

Soon after Pleasant Hill and Union Village closed in 1910, three more eastern societies closed and combined with other societies: Enfield, Connecticut, in 1917; Enfield, New Hampshire, in 1918; and Harvard, Massachusetts, in 1919. So surely the South Union leaders were not surprised when Elder Walter Shepard of Mount Lebanon (as New Lebanon was now called) came to close South Union and to arrange for the sale of the property. It was clear to all that it was no longer feasible for two men and six women to try to operate a farm of 4,113 acres with hired help.

Given a choice of a lifetime home in the Mother Society or a gift of $10,000, only one—Elder Logan Johns—chose to go east.

Johns's decision was in keeping with the fact that he was the last of the Johns family that had played a prominent role throughout the 115-year history of South Union. It was also a realistic decision, for Elder Logan was a feeble man of eighty. Accompanied by the hired farm manager, Joe Wallace, Johns traveled to New York in a train drawing room. Two years later, in December of 1924, Logan Johns of the Logan County Shakers was buried in the cemetery of the Mother Society.

Josie Bridges, who had become mentally ill, was taken east. The other six accepted the money and moved into the world's society.

Interestingly enough, Lizzie Simmons and William Bates married. Their combined sum of $20,000 provided them a comfortable living the rest of their lives. The eastern and

South Union ministries agreed that Bates should have the Shaker automobile. One wonders whether Elders Walter and Logan thought of it as a wedding gift to William and Lizzie.

Josie Thrall and Mary Wann moved three miles away to homes of friends in Auburn, and Mary later moved to Florida. Miss Annie Farmer and her mother moved to Louisville.

Josie Thrall and William Bates died in 1931. Lizzie Bates died in 1933.

Several of the South Union Shakers, notably Sabrina Whitmore, had left a year or so before the dissolution and did not share in the financial settlement.

The two-day sale was held late in September of 1922. To be sold were the contents of all the buildings, the livestock, and an unusually large collection of tools and farm implements. The large farm was subdivided and sold in sixty farms ranging from 25 to 150 acres each, fifteen 5-acre tracts, and one 75-acre tract having most of the large brick buildings. Sold separately were the hotel and store building located at the railroad station.

With the closing of South Union and Pleasant Hill, active Shakerism in Kentucky came to an end.

Bibliographical Note

THE KENTUCKY SHAKERS, like Shakers everywhere, kept a full written record of all aspects of their communal life. Given to order and self-discipline it was natural for those charged with keeping the family house journals and account books to be consistent in making their daily entries. There was also the awareness that each local society was accountable to the head eastern ministry who would inspect the records periodically.

The leading elder in each society was responsible for the Church family journal which contained reports on the weather, important events, admission as well as decease or departure of members, travels of the ministry and trustees, visitors, farming and building operations, industries, domestic concerns, and proceedings of society meetings as well as society appointments. Usually included was the annual census giving date and place of birth of the members and the date of their joining the society.

More detailed records of the various industries were kept in separate account books. For example the 1814 South Union fulling mill book contains each patron's name, the yardage of his order, the dye color, and the total cost. Such specific entries were protection against any later complaint from the outside customers.

Other account books contain the expenditures and receipts relating to the grinding of wheat and corn, sawing of timber, and to the sales of such items as flour, seeds, herbs, brooms, garden produce, preserves, and livestock. Further business records were kept in special books by deacons and deaconesses.

Letters form a large part of all Shaker manuscript records. Being scattered from southern Kentucky to Maine, the leaders of the nineteen major communities depended greatly on correspondence to keep in touch one with the other. The gap between the official ministerial visits was bridged by ministerial letters. Those sent from the parent ministry to the Kentucky societies were largely letters of encouragement and information relating to changes in policy or practice. Those sent east reported the condition of the particular society and perhaps recounted an exceptional event or asked advice on some matter. Letters from other ministries were often read aloud in the society meetings. Copies of particularly significant letters were sometimes bound into a letter book.

Not only letters but the journals of the early leaders and other personal accounts were often copied in entirety or excerpts were written into other records. "Church Journal A" (1804–1836) kept at South Union contains the autobiography of John Rankin, Sr., (1746–1834) as well as entries from the early Ohio journal of Benjamin Seth Youngs and from a Pleasant Hill Church journal kept by B. B. Dunlavy.

Among the Kentucky Shaker manuscripts are several significant accounts kept by individuals. Among these are Thomas Jefferson Shannon's account of a South Union trading voyage made to New Orleans (October 6, 1831–February 1832), Eldress Nancy E. Moore's South Union journal "Incidents concerning the War" (1861–1864), and a journal kept on a trip in 1869 to the eastern societies by the joint ministry of Pleasant Hill and South Union.

Both societies had manuscript hymnals which contained either simple texts or texts accompanied by the tune written in alphabetical notation. Selections copied into the hymnals were often composed within the society, some by inspiration. Hymns from other societies were often received in letters. The name of the composer and the society or just the society name might follow the hymns.

Sermons, addresses, essays, and documents are also found in the Shaker manuscript collections.

Primary material related to both Pleasant Hill and South Union is part of the extensive American Shaker collection at

Western Reserve Historical Society in Cleveland. According to the society's "Guide to Shaker Manuscripts" (1974), there are 14 volumes and 171 items from Pleasant Hill and 73 volumes and 368 items from South Union. Letters compose a large portion of the items. In addition, there are miscellaneous pieces such as maps, a list of books lent from the South Union library (1861–1863) and a perpetual almanac by B. S. Youngs, Pleasant Hill, 1811.

In Kentucky the primary source material concerning Pleasant Hill is located in the Harrodsburg Historical Society and in the Filson Club. The combined sources cover the history of Pleasant Hill from 1815 through 1917, seven years after the official close of the colony. Manuscripts of all types are represented in the collections.

The largest collection of South Union primary material is located in the manuscript department of the Kentucky Library at Western Kentucky University. The Church journals cover the years 1804–1917. Other journals and account books supplement the church records and carry the society records through 1916. To expedite the reader's use of the records, the major manuscripts have been typed and bound. Some have been indexed.

At the Filson Club the outstanding Shaker collection is the Bohon Collection. At the Kentucky Library the main ones are the Coke, Rodes, and Wallace collections.

The Kentucky Shakers not only wrote, but they published. Most of the early works were theological, such as Benjamin Seth Youngs's *Testimony of Christ's Second Appearing* (Lebanon, Ohio, 1808) and John Dunlavy's *Manifesto* (Pleasant Hill, 1818). Two works that are helpful in a study of the early history of the western Shakers are B. S. Youngs's *Transactions of the Ohio Mob or an Expedition against the Shakers* (Miami Country, Ohio, 1810) and Richard McNemar's *The Kentucky Revival* (Cincinnati, Ohio, 1807).

Beginning in 1871 the American Shakers began publishing a monthly periodical, *The Shaker*. Changed in title to the *Manifesto* in 1883, the magazine ceased publication in December

1899. The magazine contains much Kentucky material in the form of monthly "Home Notes," poems, articles, hymns, and sermons.

Secondary sources relating to the Kentucky Shakers include: Thomas D. Clark and Gerald Ham, *Pleasant Hill and Its Shakers* (Pleasant Hill, Ky., 1968); Thomas D. Clark, *Pleasant Hill Shakers in the Civil War* (Pleasant Hill, Ky., 1972); Julia Neal, *By Their Fruits: The Story of South Union* (Chapel Hill, N.C., 1947; reprint, Philadelphia, 1975); Julia Neal, ed., *The Journal of Eldress Nancy* (Nashville, Tenn., 1963); Samuel Thomas and James Thomas, *The Simple Spirit: A Pictorial History of Pleasant Hill* (Pleasant Hill, Ky., 1973).

Articles on the Kentucky Shakers have appeared in the *Filson Club Historical Quarterly* and in the *Register* of the Kentucky Historical Society.

A 1976 monograph, *Trade with the World's People: A Shaker Album*, by Susan Jackson Keig has been published by the Becket Paper Company, Hamilton, Ohio.

Anyone interested in all things Shaker would do well to consult Mary Richmond's two-volume annotated bibliography *Shaker Literature* (Hanover, N.H., 1976).